WHAT MOST PARENTS AREN'T TELLING YOU

What Most Parents Aren't Telling You:
Four Insights About Parents that Should Radically Impact Your Ministry

Published by Orange in partnership with Parent Cue
thinkorange.com and parentcue.org

5870 Charlotte Lane, Suite 300
Cumming, GA 30040

All rights reserved. Except for brief excerpts for review purposes, no part of this book may be reproduced or used in any form without written permission from the publisher. Other Orange and Parent Cue products are available online and direct from the publisher. Visit our websites at www.ParentCue.org and www.ThinkOrange.com for more resources like these.

To request permissions, contact the publisher at partnersupport@rethinkgroup.org.

Copyright © 2022 The reThink Group. All rights reserved.

ISBN: 978-1-63570-190-6

Design by: Elizabeth Hildreth, Hannah Joiner
Writing Team: Kristen Ivy, Leah Jennings, Mitchell McGhee, Lauren Sellers
Research Team: Darren Kizer, Terry Linhart, Tyler Greenway, Eric Shieh, Mark Szabo

Printed in the USA 08/10/2022

First Edition

2 3 4 5 6 7 8 9 10 11

What Most Parents Aren't Telling You

AN ORANGE REPORT
PRODUCED WITH PARENT CUE

Four Insights About Parents That Should Radically Impact Your Ministry

"But however the forms of family life have changed and the number expanded, the role of the family has remained constant and it continues to be the major institution through which children pass en route to adulthood."

— Bernice Weissbourd

Before

Why Now is the Time to Listen 06
Introduction by Carey Nieuwhof

The Influence of a Family 08
A Preface by Reggie Joiner

A Note from Kristen Ivy 10

Terms 12
What We Mean

Sections

#01 What Parents Want 15

#02 What Parents Fear 31

#03 What Parents Feel 49

#04 Where Parents Go For Help 69

#05 Distinctions by Race and Ethnicity 92

#06 Distinctions by Family Structure 108

After

Different Ways to Read This Book 116

Methodology 118
How We Conducted Our Research

Notes 121

Acknowledgments 126
The People Who Made This

Project Partners 127
The People Who Made it Possible

Introduction: Why Now is the Time to Listen
by Carey Nieuwhof

→ "When we stay curious, with humility about the possibility that we haven't figured it out, then there is more that can be discovered." —*Francesca Gino*

The thought of leading the Church forward might feel impossible right now, but it isn't. And fortunately, there's help.

Rather than getting exhausted by what's changing (which is so easy to do), what if you and I got curious about what's changing instead?

That's why I'm so excited about the project Orange and Parent Cue have created with What Most Parents Aren't Telling You. This research is an honest dive into what parents are feeling, thinking, and in need of at this moment in time.

Here's the bottom line: Family needs are changing, and the Church needs to figure out how to respond to those changes.

Through numerous studies over the past decade, parents have said they want a congregation that's supportive of their family life—one that offers practical help for their role as a parent.

The new research reveals that:

41% of respondents desire resources to better understand their child's phase of life

38% of respondents were looking for resources to enable better conversations with their kid

63% of respondents wish someone would provide family experiences they can attend with their kid

As a leader, you likely hear from a select group of parents a lot. But my guess is sometimes what you're hearing gets in the way of what you may need to hear even more—like the thoughts of many parents, and the parents and children you're hoping to reach.

One of my hopes is that as you read this research, you'll gain some fresh insights. You'll have an opportunity to hear from voices that may not always be the loudest, and yet they may also be some of the most essential if we want to build churches that reach those who aren't coming yet. You and I have an opportunity in front of us to nurture the faith and the future potential of a generation. Parents matter, and connecting to the church matters now more than ever.

You ready? Here's to listening and learning...

Carey Nieuwhof

Parent of 3, pastor, speaker, podcaster, and best-selling author of *Didn't See It Coming* and *Lasting Impact*

Preface: The Influence of a Family
by Reggie Joiner

→ What happens at home is more important than what happens at church. I know… bold statement. But after 40+ years of ministry, I still believe this to be true.

What happens at home is more important because kids spend more time at home.

Now, this doesn't mean as leaders we won't have influence, it just means there are others who have more. Even with the kids who attended church consistently, at best I would only have about 40 hours with them every year. That's only 40 hours to help a kid or student understand everything they need to know about God, the Bible, and life.

The amount of time the average parent gets to spend with their child in a single year is 3,000 hours. It's staggering, honestly, when you simply consider the potential of 40 hours versus 3,000 hours you can see why what happens at home is more important.

What happens at home is more important because parents will have lifelong influence.

I remember those early years of ministry, being invited to every sort of milestone event—ball games, graduations, and even officiating weddings—only to realize that after spending countless hours investing in these students' lives, I still only played a small part in their worlds.

It can be tempting to start believing you have more—maybe even better—influence than a kid or teenager's parent. But remember, a mom, dad, grandparent, foster parent, or step-parent has been with a kid for a long time—maybe since the beginning. They've seen more, loved more, cried more, hoped more, and been hurt more by this child than you ever will.

<u>Regardless of their issues, baggage, and brokenness, every parent wants to be a better parent.</u> No matter what you think about parents—conservative, liberal, strict, and laid-back alike—the reality is they have more influence than you do. Think about it this way: At best, you will have temporary influence. By default, a parent has lifelong influence.

If you want to help parents win, you have to care about parents.

It's not enough to just show up for parents because we have to. We don't just show up because we want influence with them, or because it's in our job description; we show up because we care about what parents care about.

Many kids and teenagers in this generation will decide how they see the Church when they see how the church treats their parent. So, what if we allow the findings of this research to inform the way we greet every parent, communicate to every parent, encourage every parent, and resource every parent? We just might find that the best thing we can do for a kid's faith is to learn how to love their parent well. Because truly, what happens at home is more important than what happens at church, and no one has more potential to influence a kid than a parent.

Reggie Joiner

Parent of 4, Grandparent of 6, CEO & Founder of Orange, Author of *Think Orange*, *Don't Miss It*, and *It's Personal*

A Note
from Kristen Ivy

→ Two weeks to flatten the curve. *Can someone send us video links we can send out to parents next Sunday? How is your team planning to do Easter this year?*

These were a few of the questions I remember pouring into our offices in the Spring of 2020. The world was preparing to plunge head-first into something no living human had experienced.

This might not seem like the ideal time to begin an in-depth research initiative on parents, but in some ways, it could not have been better timed. The past two years have been an opportunity to break free from established patterns, listen, and recalibrate. So, as the U.S. census team set out to collect 2020 census data, Orange and Parent Cue commissioned what would become a sixteen-month series of studies with Arbor Research Group to better understand the reality of parents and their relationship with faith communities in the U.S.

From the outset, our goal was to discover as much as possible about U.S. parents, from a representative sample of states and regions, income levels, races and ethnicities, family structures, and genders. We hoped to provide ministry leaders with insights about what parents want, what parents fear, how parents feel, and where parents go for help. By gathering this information, we wanted to fuel conversations about how ministries and families can work together to give kids and teenagers a stronger and more vibrant faith, and a better future.

Some of the aims of the study evolved over the course of four surveys and two listening sessions. We added, for example, a group of parents who self-reported as committed Christians from a range of denominations and affiliations. This group highlights some places where Christian parents may differ from the general population of parents overall. More of the specific methodology is listed at the end of this book.

What we have learned from the findings so far both confirms and challenges a number of beliefs. In many ways, it also raises questions. In order to release the findings in a timely manner, this report does not provide many directives or applications. Instead, our team has highlighted places within the research that feel like moments to pause, reflect, and consider what parents seem to be saying by their responses.

<u>You picked up this book because you care about the faith and future of the next generation.</u> So do we. And we have a shared belief that the Church is positioned to answer the call to support parents and caregivers as we build ministries for kids and teenagers. This study is an exercise in listening deeply to what parents have to say about their own experience. <u>As you read the findings within, I have one request: Will you read with a filter of radical empathy?</u>

Will you listen to the voice of thousands of parents who took time to share their hopes, fears, and experiences as a part of this study, and will you believe them?

Will you set aside a culturally normative framework—a bias that makes it so easy to blame parents, judge parents, and dismiss parents? And will you instead read with a counter-cultural lens—one that trusts parents.

This study did not set out to help leaders learn how to fix the family. Instead, we set out to listen to every caregiver, in order to learn how to better serve every family. As we look to the days ahead, many leaders have made the observation, "Now is not the season for the Church to return to what was. Now is the season to reimagine what the Church will be." We hope this project can fuel our collective imagination.

Kristen Ivy

Parent of 3, President of Orange and Parent Cue,
Author of *It's Just a Phase: So Don't Miss It* and the
18-series *Phase Guides* for parents

Terms
What We Mean

Parent

The findings in this study use the term "parent" to refer to any adult who is consistently tasked with the responsibility of raising a young person under the age of 26. It may refer to a guardian, grandparent, stepparent, foster parent, or any number of adult-to-child relationships in which the adult has consistent caregiver responsibilities.

Kid

The findings in this study use the term "kid" to refer to any young person under the age of 26 who is the object of parental caretaking. This may refer to a person who is the biological, foster, or adopted responsibility of a parent. This study found that the term "kid" was most commonly used by parents when referring to a young person under their care, regardless of that young person's age—although words like "children" and "adult children" were also common.

All Parents

The terms "all parents" and "general population of parents" refer to a randomly selected, nationally representative sample of 1,464 U.S. nonreligious and "religious but not practicing" parents. This group participated in a survey in June 2021. For more detailed information, see the section titled "Methodology."

Christian Parents

The term "Christian parents" most often refers to a randomly selected, nationally representative sample of 1,269 U.S. parents who all consider themselves to be "a committed Christian." This group participated in a survey in February 2022. When the term "follow up" is used in Christian parents, it refers to a second, randomly selected, similar sample of 800 U.S. parents who responded to a follow-up survey in March 2022. Any follow-up data is separately identified in footnotes. For more detailed information, see the section titled "Methodology."

"Caring about the welfare of children and shaming parents are mutually exclusive endeavors."

— Brené Brown

No one is full
of more false hope
than a parent who
brings a chair to
the beach.

Section #01

WHAT PARENTS WANT

→ You don't have to look far to recognize a growing number of adults view their parenting role as a key element of their identity. Many parents, whether athletes, musicians, pastors, or social influencers talk about their parenting as an important aspect of their life and purpose.

One Pew Research Center report found that 52% of millennials say being a good parent is "one of the most important things" in life.[1] Millennial parents, especially dads, also report spending more time with their children than previous generations of parents. More than half (57%) of fathers now say parenting is *extremely important* to their identity, only one percentage point less than mothers. And fathers now spend three times as much time with their children as they did two generations ago.[2]

As parents place an increasingly high value on their parenting, they also feel escalating pressure to parent well. Social media undoubtedly contributes to some of this pressure. One study from the popular parenting site *BabyCenter* found that 80% of millennial moms said it's important to be "the perfect mom," largely due to the desires to live up to what they see online.[3] But parents report other sources of pressure as well. Nearly three-fourths (72%) of parents report wanting their own parents to think they are doing a good job of parenting, and 93% of married or cohabiting parents say it matters a lot that their spouse or partner sees them as a good parent.[4] In addition to pressure from social media, comparison, and the perception of others, many parents feel an intrinsic burden to do right by their kids. One study out of Boston College demonstrates this deep-seated intrinsic burden, revealing that three-fourths of fathers say they wish they could spend more time with their kids.[5]

In a generation of parents who want to raise kids well, and feel significant pressure to do so, parents need new levels of support in order to provide for the physical, emotional, mental, and spiritual well-being of the children and teenagers in their homes. The pending question is this: Where will parents find the support network they need as they navigate their parenting journey? In order to build effective support systems, ministry leaders will need to first understand more about what parents value.

Section 01   What Parents Want   What Most Parents Aren't Telling You

What Parents Want for Their Kids

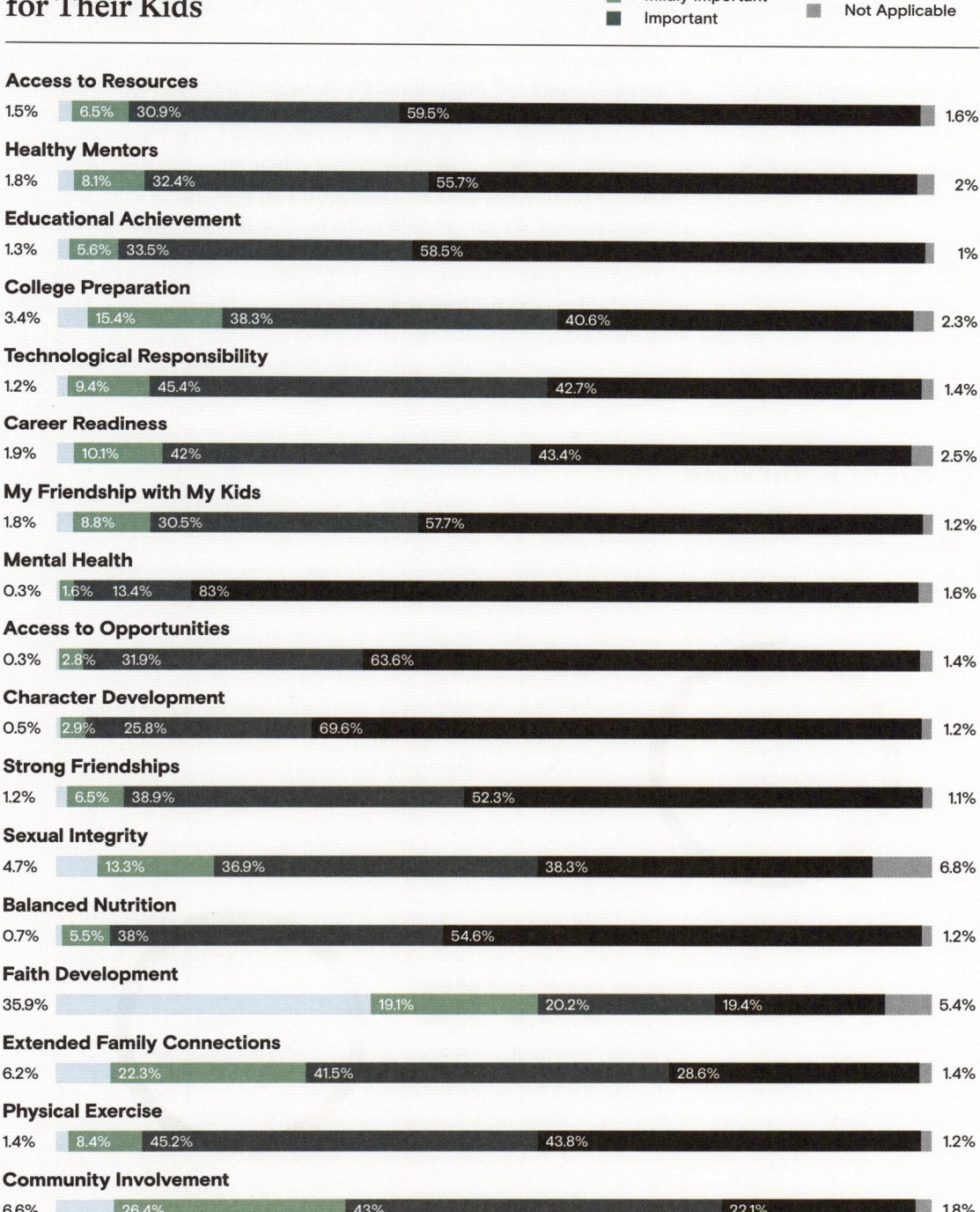

Legend:
- Not Important
- Mildly Important
- Important
- Extremely Important
- Not Applicable

Access to Resources
1.5% | 6.5% | 30.9% | 59.5% | 1.6%

Healthy Mentors
1.8% | 8.1% | 32.4% | 55.7% | 2%

Educational Achievement
1.3% | 5.6% | 33.5% | 58.5% | 1%

College Preparation
3.4% | 15.4% | 38.3% | 40.6% | 2.3%

Technological Responsibility
1.2% | 9.4% | 45.4% | 42.7% | 1.4%

Career Readiness
1.9% | 10.1% | 42% | 43.4% | 2.5%

My Friendship with My Kids
1.8% | 8.8% | 30.5% | 57.7% | 1.2%

Mental Health
0.3% | 1.6% | 13.4% | 83% | 1.6%

Access to Opportunities
0.3% | 2.8% | 31.9% | 63.6% | 1.4%

Character Development
0.5% | 2.9% | 25.8% | 69.6% | 1.2%

Strong Friendships
1.2% | 6.5% | 38.9% | 52.3% | 1.1%

Sexual Integrity
4.7% | 13.3% | 36.9% | 38.3% | 6.8%

Balanced Nutrition
0.7% | 5.5% | 38% | 54.6% | 1.2%

Faith Development
35.9% | 19.1% | 20.2% | 19.4% | 5.4%

Extended Family Connections
6.2% | 22.3% | 41.5% | 28.6% | 1.4%

Physical Exercise
1.4% | 8.4% | 45.2% | 43.8% | 1.2%

Community Involvement
6.6% | 26.4% | 43% | 22.1% | 1.8%

n = 1,464 U.S. parents with kids 0–25, June 2021

Section 01   What Parents Want   What Most Parents Aren't Telling You

→ Parents need new levels of support in order to provide for the physical, emotional, mental, and spiritual well-being of the children and teenagers in their homes.

Raising Humans with the Future in Mind

Every caregiver places a high value on things that seem significant for their child or teenager's future. As part of this study, parents rated seventeen separate parenting categories on a scale of not important to extremely important. More than 65% of the general population of parents valued *every aspect* as *important* or *extremely important*—except one: faith development (coming in at 39.6%.) The high level of importance parents place on all aspects of parenting stands out as particularly notable. It reinforces the idea that parents feel substantial value and pressure related to their caregiving duties. Consider this. The average parent feels responsible for delivering adequate to excellent support for the young person in their home in 17 different areas ranging from physical exercise to healthy mentors to career readiness. It's a lot to keep up with!

Levels of Enthusiasm

How parents rate all 17 parenting values on average.

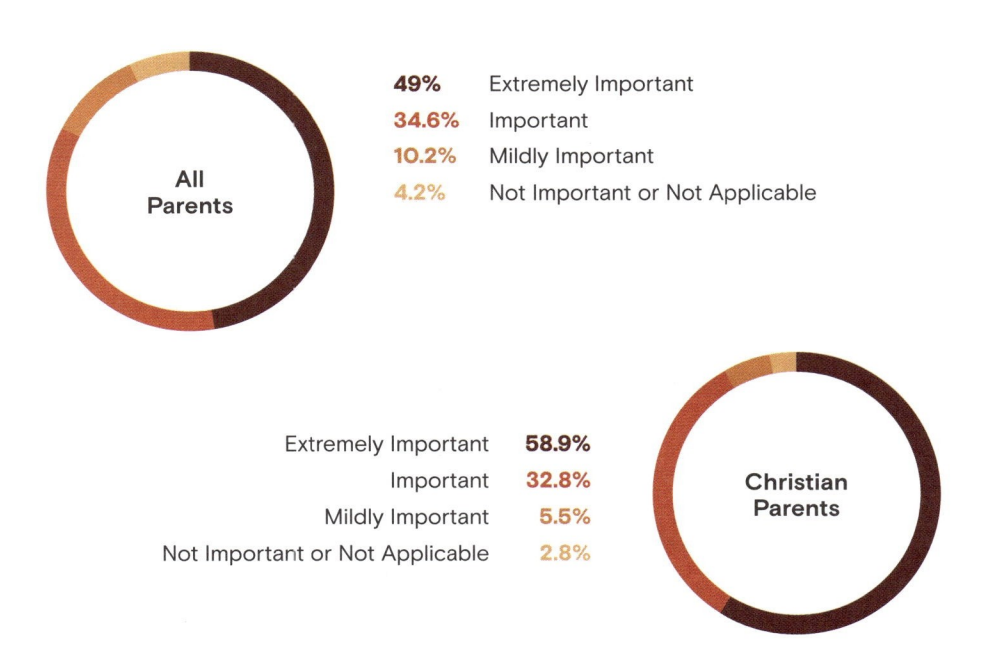

All Parents

- **49%** Extremely Important
- **34.6%** Important
- **10.2%** Mildly Important
- **4.2%** Not Important or Not Applicable

Christian Parents

- Extremely Important **58.9%**
- Important **32.8%**
- Mildly Important **5.5%**
- Not Important or Not Applicable **2.8%**

n = 1,464 U.S. parents with kids 0–25, June 2021
n = 1,269 U.S. Christian parents with kids 0–25, February 2022

When it comes to priorities, parents place the greatest value on mental health (96.4%), access to opportunities (95.8%), and character development (95.5%) by rating them *important* to *extremely important*. Parents also consistently place both physical exercise (88.9%) and nutrition (92.7%) high on their list, indicating a significant value for their kids' physical well-being.

Levels of Enthusiasm

It might not be a surprise, but parents who identify themselves as "committed Christians" place a much higher value on faith development than the general population. Most Christian parents (94%) say their kids' faith is *important* to *extremely important* compared to only 40% of the general population. What might be surprising, however, is the elevated value Christian parents place on *every aspect* of their parenting. For each of the parenting values included in our study, Christian parents selected *extremely important* 10% more often than the general parenting population. In contrast, the general parenting population selected *not important* more than twice as often as Christian parents. Given the margin between all parents (general population) and committed Christian parents, it begs the question: What is it about valuing faith that elevates the value of everything else? One might wonder if Christian parents are aware of a connection between faith and everything else. It may also underscore an opportunity for ministry leaders to gain parents' attention when they connect faith with other highly valued aspects of parenting.

→ In the top three responses, Christian parents don't differ from the general population in what they say matters most.

What Parents Want Most

While committed Christian parents differ from the general population in the level of importance they place on their parenting, both groups consistently prioritize the same parenting values in almost every area. In the top three responses, Christian parents don't differ from the general population in what they say matters most.

→ The three lowest values for Christian parents were among the lowest five for the general population.

All Parents' Top Three
#1 Mental Health
#2 Access to Opportunities
#3 Character Development

Christian Parents' Top Three
#1 Mental Health
#2 Access to Opportunities
#3 Character Development

Likewise, the three lowest values for Christian parents were among the lowest five for the general population. Both groups ranked community involvement, college preparation, and sexual integrity in their bottom five. The general population also ranked faith and extended family relationships comparatively low. It's important to note, however, the majority of parents in both groups still rate even their lowest values *important* to *extremely important*. In other words, there is no such thing as an insignificant parenting value.

→ There is no such thing as an insignificant parenting value.

Section 01 What Parents Want What Most Parents Aren't Telling You

Parents Differ in their Value for Faith and Relationships

The percent of parents who say faith and relationships are *important* or *very important*.

	All Parents	Christian Parents
Relationships (mentors, my friendship with my kid, peer friendships, extended family, community)	80.5%	90.7%
Faith	39.6%	94.3%

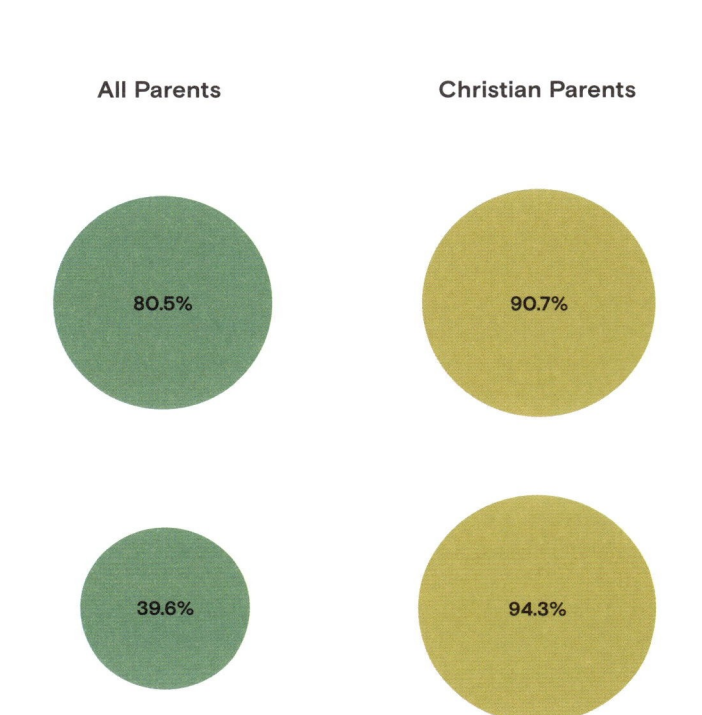

n = 1,464 U.S. parents with kids 0–25, June 2021
n = 1,269 U.S. Christian parents with kids 0–25, February 2022

Where the Gaps Widen

The most striking contrast between Christian parents and the general population of parents is, of course, how they prioritize faith. Christian parents rate faith development as the fourth most important parenting value, just below character development.

Perhaps the second most noteworthy distinction between Christian parents and the general population is that Christian parents generally prioritize relationships at a higher level. Christian parents say mentors, parental friendship, peer friendship, extended family, and community are *important* to *extremely important* (+10% more often than the general population.) And 90.7% of Christian parents specifically prioritize extended family relationships, as compared to 80% of the general parent population. Conversely, there were no notable differences between the two groups related to career, health, or character.

The Importance of Character

Standing out as a high value for every parent, over 95% of both the general population of parents and Christian parents say character development is *important* to *extremely important* for their kids. In their responses, parents prioritize character development third-highest in the list of fifteen parenting values. Over 80% of the general population of parents report feeling supported in this area—while nearly 90% of Christian parents feel supported in this area. Let's explore what parents mean by "character."[6]

When asked to respond to a series of questions designed to evaluate parents' perception of 39 potential character traits, the majority of parents indicated that *all* 39 character qualities were *important*. In fact, the lowest-scoring value was still selected as *important* by 61.3% of parents. From this set, 15 character qualities stood out above the rest, having no negative correlations. Parents demonstrated consistent confidence in importance, relevance, and meaning for all 15 of the top character traits.

---

15 Character Traits Every Parent Values:

- honesty
- compassion
- peace
- respect
- knowledge
- love
- forgiveness
- trust
- responsibility
- self-control
- confidence
- wisdom
- kindness
- commitment
- integrity

n = 571 U.S. parents with kids 0–25, November/December 2020

When compared to the general population of parents, Christian parents selected the same top three character qualities from 39 options—with one notable distinction.

All Parents' Top Three
#1 Honesty
#2 Trust
#3 Love

Christian Parents' Top Three
#1 Honesty
#2 Faith
#3 Love

→ Christian parents selected the same top three character values from 39 options—with one notable distinction.

In their response to character traits, Christian parents were more alike than unlike the general population of parents. But Christian parents favored faith and obedience more than the general population by a significant margin. Both faith and obedience were notably absent from the top fifteen character traits for the general population.

Female parents named many of the character traits *important* more often than male parents. And parents who were older tended to rank conviction, humility, and respect higher than parents who were younger. Parents who were younger tended to favor uniqueness more than parents who were older.

Parents Differ in their Value for Faith and Obedience

The percent of parents who say faith and obedience are *important* or *very important*.

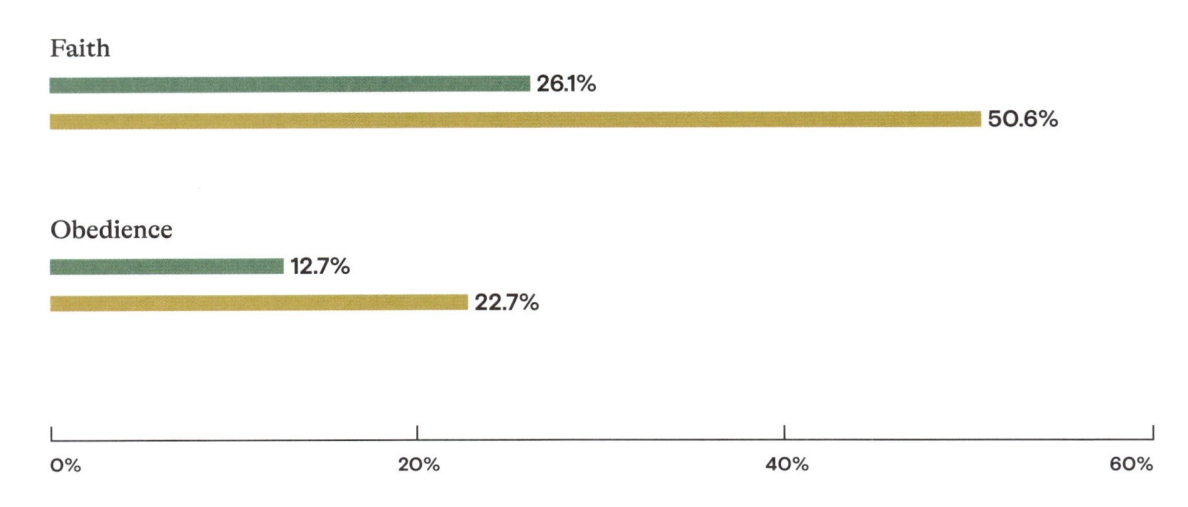

■ All Parents
■ Christian Parents

Faith
All Parents: 26.1%
Christian Parents: 50.6%

Obedience
All Parents: 12.7%
Christian Parents: 22.7%

n = 1,464 U.S. parents with kids 0–25, June 2021
n = 1,269 U.S. Christian parents with kids 0–25, February 2022

Every group of parents, regardless of demographic, consistently prioritize the transferring of character to their kids as one of their top parenting values. Christian parents rate the importance of almost all character qualities higher than the general population, and those Christians who attend church almost every week—or at least twice a month—rate character qualities higher than those who attend less frequently. This, again, raises some questions: <u>What is it about faith, and participation in a faith community, that correlates with an elevated value of character? Are Christian parents able to articulate why they value character more highly than the general population? And, do Christian parents feel they are able to help their kids see the connection between faith and character in an everyday context?</u>

→ What is it about faith and participation in a faith community that correlates with an elevated value of character?

The Importance of Faith & Church

Christian parents place a high value on faith for their kids to the extent that 94.3% say faith is *important* or *extremely important*. In a 2020 study, Barna Research also revealed that 58% of highly engaged Christian parents say children's programming is the primary reason they chose their current church. With findings like these, we might expect that family programming will automatically gain influence in a community filled with parents who are seeking support for their kids' faith formation.

While the percentage of committed Christian parents who value their kids' faith is especially encouraging, there is a gap between those who value faith for their kids and those who consistently attend church programming. Compared to 94.3% of parents who say faith is *important* or *extremely important*, only 63% rated the following statement as very true: "Consistent connection to a faith community is an essential part of our family." More than one out of three committed Christians rated this statement only *mildly* or *moderately true*.

Attendance at weekly religious services follows the same pattern. Committed Christian parents say their attendance at weekly religious services is inconsistent, with 61.7% of parents claiming they attend services almost every week. More than 17% of committed Christian parents claim they attend once a month.[7]

This gap may indicate a shift from previous generations of parents. In 2010, a study by Orange and Barna Research found that having children was a catalyst for 5% of parents to become active in church for the first time, for 20% of parents to reconnect with church after a long period of not attending, and for 30% of parents to become more active in church than they already were.[8] The new questions seem to be: <u>How does parenting impact church attendance today? Are some Christian parents reevaluating the value of church attendance for their kids' faith? And, if so, how might this impact the future of children's' and youth ministries?</u>

→ There is a gap between those who value faith for their kids and those who consistently attend church programming.

It's worth noting that faith is still the fourth-highest value even for the most committed Christian parent—just behind mental health, access to opportunities, and character development, and within one percentage point of healthy friendships and balanced nutrition. This illustrates

→ While Christian parents value faith, it isn't the only thing they value when it comes to parenting.

→ Parents may require new support in their effort to nurture faith development even beyond attendance at weekly services.

that while Christian parents value faith, it isn't the only thing they value when it comes to parenting. This observation may provide some insight for leaders exploring the questions above. While Christian parents still value a faith community, many parents may find themselves juggling competing priorities that also impact their kids' future.

Given the decline in church and parish attendance, it may come as no surprise to many ministry leaders that even some of the most committed Christian parents are feeling a lack of support in nurturing their kid or teenager's faith development. More than half (54%) say they are *well-supported* in the area of faith development. By comparison, 15.1% of the general parenting population report feeling *well-supported* in their child's faith development, and 13.9% report feeling *unsupported*. We will return in Section Three to the support gap for parents wishing to nurture their kids' faith development. But for now, faith leaders may want to take note. Parents may require new support in their effort to nurture faith development even beyond attendance at weekly services.

The Value of Faith is Very Strong for Christian Parents

94.3% of committed Christian parents say faith is *important* to *extremely important*.

→ Those same parents rank faith fourth—just behind mental health, access to opportunities, and character development, and within one percentage point of healthy friendships and balanced nutrition.

94.3%

The Value of Church is Less Strong for Christian Parents

Survey Statement
Consistent connection to a faith community is an essential part of our family.

- 63% Very True
- 25.1% Moderately True
- 10.7% Mildly True
- 1.2% Untrue

Church Attendance Mirrors Christian Parents' Value for Church

Survey Question
How often do you and your family attend church or parish services?

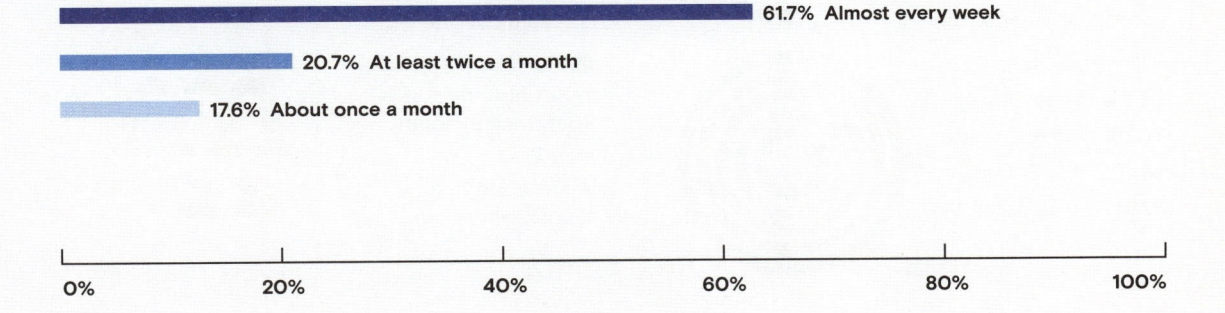

- 61.7% Almost every week
- 20.7% At least twice a month
- 17.6% About once a month

n = 1,269 U.S. Christian parents with kids 0–25, February 2022

Section 01 · What Parents Want · What Most Parents Aren't Telling You

What Parents Want at Every Phase

Some of the most significant findings of this study are the ways in which a parent's experience changes as a child moves from birth through preschool, elementary, middle, and finally high school.

The top three parenting values—mental health, access to opportunities, and character development—remain consistent in every phase with one exception. Parents raising six- and seven-year-old children prioritize balanced nutrition above these three values, making it the highest priority parenting value for that phase. The lowest three values for the general population remain consistently faith development, community involvement, and extended family connection in every phase.

While the highest and lowest values stay consistently high or low across every phase, each value does shift in importance from age group to age group. Below we highlight the phase where each specific value reached its peak level of importance.

For those who work with
→ **Preschoolers**

Summary
Parents rate access to resources highest in the first three years of parenting, and friendship with their children highest when their child is four and five years old.

Parental Value Peak with ages 0–3
- Access to Resources

Parental Value Peak with ages 4–5
- Friendship with My Kids

Notable
Parents of Preschoolers say friendship with their kid is *more important* to *extremely important* than parents of other ages.

91.1% Preschool
89.7% Elementary
86.5% Middle School
88.6% High School
87.3% Young Adult

For those who work with
→ **Elementary**

Summary
Parents rate education, nutrition, and community highest when their kid is six and seven years old, and character highest when their kid is upper elementary.

Parental Value Peak with ages 6–7
- Educational Achievement
- Balanced Nutrition
- Community Involvement

Parental Value Peak with ages 8–11
- Character Development

Notable
Christian Parents of six- and seven-year-olds attend church most often.

18.8% report attending at least twice a month
69.9% report attending almost every week

n = 1,269 U.S. Christian parents with kids 0–25, February 2022

Section 01 — What Parents Want — What Most Parents Aren't Telling You

For those who work with
→ **Middle Schoolers**

Summary
Parents rate faith development, character, and community involvement high when their kid is twelve to fifteen years old.

Parental Value Peak with ages 12–15
- Character Development
- Faith Development
- Community Involvement

Notable
Parents in the general population value faith most when their kid is twelve to fifteen years old.

30.7% Not Important
20.2% Mildly Important
23.5% Important
25.6% Extremely Important

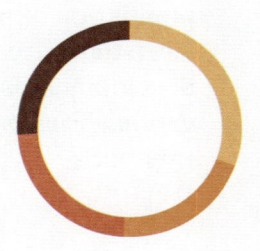

For those who work with
→ **High Schoolers**

Summary
Parents rate education, college prep, technological responsibility, friendships, sexual integrity, and faith development highest when their kid is sixteen to eighteen years old.

Parental Value Peak with ages 16–18
- Educational Achievement
- College Preparation
- Technological Responsibility
- Sexual Integrity
- Strong Friendships
- Faith Development

Notable
Parents place an increasing level of importance on their kids' mental health as they get older.

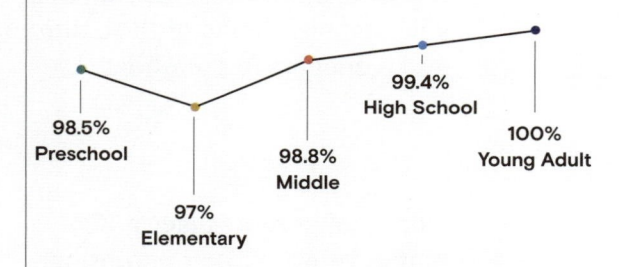

- 98.5% Preschool
- 97% Elementary
- 98.8% Middle
- 99.4% High School
- 100% Young Adult

Percent of parents who say mental health is *important* to *very important*.

For those who work with
→ **Young Adults**

Summary
Parents of nineteen to twenty-three-year-olds rate healthy mentors, career readiness, mental health, extended family connections, and physical exercise highest.

Parental Value Peak with ages 19–23
- Healthy Mentors
- Career Readiness
- Mental Health
- Physical Exercise
- Extended Family Connections

Notable
Parents of sixteen through eighteen-year-olds value mental health.

100%

12.8% Important
87.2% Very Important

n = 1,464 U.S. parents with kids 0–25, June 2021

Key Findings: What Parents Want

01
Parents need new levels of support in order to provide for the physical, emotional, mental, and spiritual well-being of the children and teenagers in their home.

02
Christian parents place a 10% higher value on their parenting than the general population. This begs the question: What is it about valuing faith that elevates the value of everything else?

03
Parents value their friendship with their kid most when their kid is four and five years old.

04
Over 95% of both the general population of parents and Christian parents say character development is *important* to *extremely important* for their kids.

05
When it comes to nurturing their kids' character, parents value three traits above all others: Honesty, Trust, and Love.

06
Compared to 94.3% of Christian parents who say faith is *important* or *extremely important*, only 63% of Christian parents say connection to a faith community is essential for their family.

07

While faith is highly valued by Christian parents, it isn't the only thing they value when it comes to parenting.

08

In the top three responses, Christian parents don't differ from the general population in what they say matters most for their kids: Mental Health, Access to Opportunities, and Character Development.

09

Christian parents of six- and seven-year-olds are most consistent in church or parish attendance.

10

Parents value faith development and community involvement highest when their kids are between twelve and fifteen years old.

11

99.4% of parents of high schoolers and 100% of parents of nineteen to twenty-three-year-olds say their kids' mental health is *important* to *extremely important*.

Don't worry, it's just
the first 40 years of
parenting that are
the hardest.

Sec

WHAT PARENTS FEAR

→ Humans worry about the things they care about. They also worry about things they can't control. Most people, for example, worry about money, job security, relationships, and health. But why do humans worry?

When asked this question, people give a number of reasons. Some say they worry to avoid disappointment; others say they worry as a distraction. Some say they worry to prevent avoidable outcomes, increase control, or mentally formulate solutions for anticipated problems. People often also cite worry as a way of showing they care.[9] So, for a generation of parents who care deeply about their kids—rating all parenting values highly, and listing "parenting" as one of the most important aspects of their identity—it should come as no shock that a majority of parents worry.

The real question is: What do parents worry about? And for those who wish to support parents: How might understanding a parent's concerns inform the way we communicate with, resource, or respond to parents in our community?

Raising Humans in an Unpredictable World

Parents worry most about the things that could impact their kids' future. When asked to rate their level of worry about a range of parenting topics, 26.4% of all parents (general population) say they worry about the given topics *often* or *all the time*. Slightly less (26.1%) say they only worry *somewhat*, and 20% say they *rarely* worry about the given topics provided. It's worth mentioning that 7 in 10 parents indicate some level of worry about *every concern* on the list. This response demonstrates the

Section 02 — What Parents Fear — What Most Parents Aren't Telling You

What Parents Worry About for Their Kids

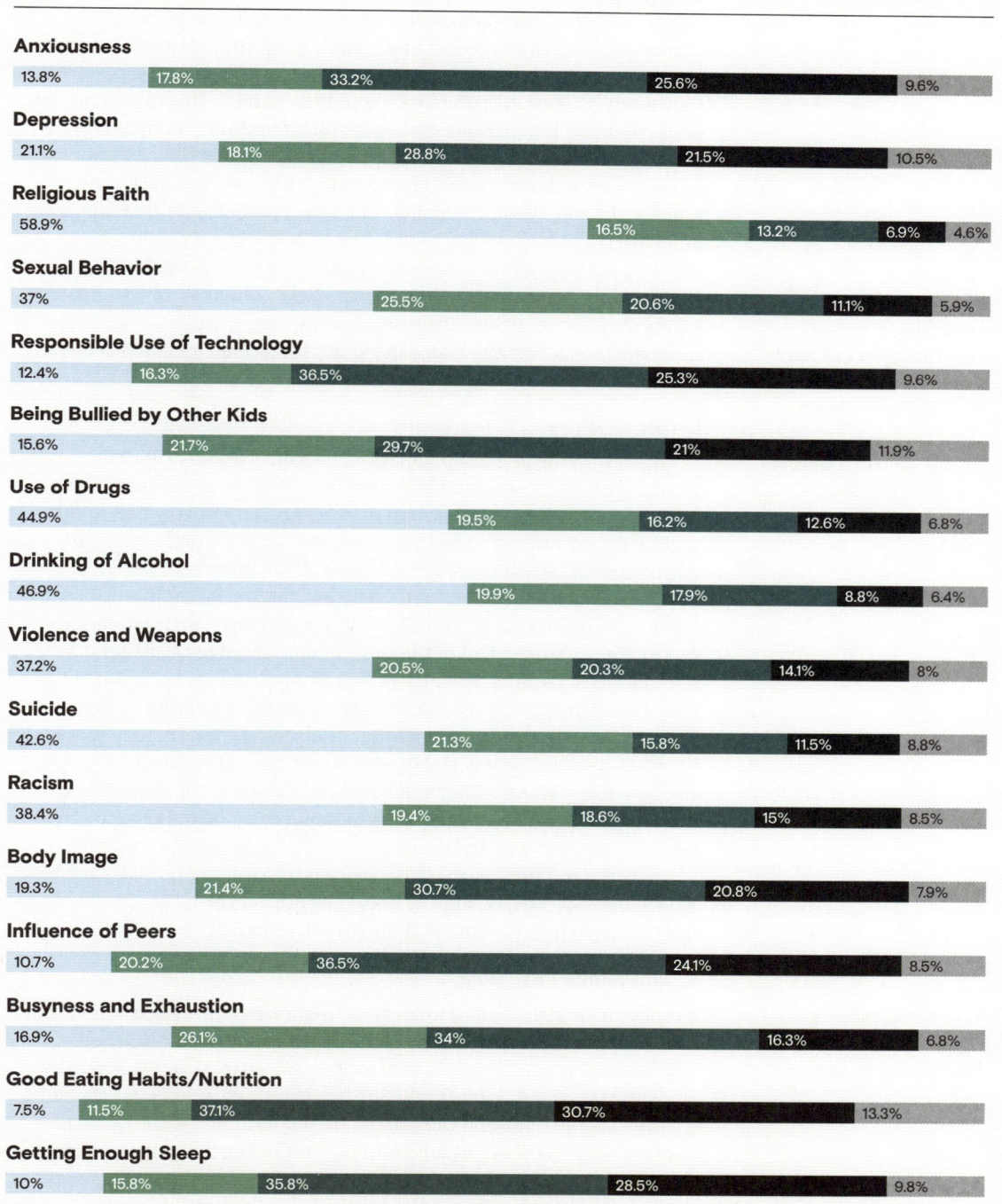

Legend: Not Important | Mildly Important | Important | Extremely Important | Not Applicable

Anxiousness
13.8% | 17.8% | 33.2% | 25.6% | 9.6%

Depression
21.1% | 18.1% | 28.8% | 21.5% | 10.5%

Religious Faith
58.9% | 16.5% | 13.2% | 6.9% | 4.6%

Sexual Behavior
37% | 25.5% | 20.6% | 11.1% | 5.9%

Responsible Use of Technology
12.4% | 16.3% | 36.5% | 25.3% | 9.6%

Being Bullied by Other Kids
15.6% | 21.7% | 29.7% | 21% | 11.9%

Use of Drugs
44.9% | 19.5% | 16.2% | 12.6% | 6.8%

Drinking of Alcohol
46.9% | 19.9% | 17.9% | 8.8% | 6.4%

Violence and Weapons
37.2% | 20.5% | 20.3% | 14.1% | 8%

Suicide
42.6% | 21.3% | 15.8% | 11.5% | 8.8%

Racism
38.4% | 19.4% | 18.6% | 15% | 8.5%

Body Image
19.3% | 21.4% | 30.7% | 20.8% | 7.9%

Influence of Peers
10.7% | 20.2% | 36.5% | 24.1% | 8.5%

Busyness and Exhaustion
16.9% | 26.1% | 34% | 16.3% | 6.8%

Good Eating Habits/Nutrition
7.5% | 11.5% | 37.1% | 30.7% | 13.3%

Getting Enough Sleep
10% | 15.8% | 35.8% | 28.5% | 9.8%

n = 1,464 U.S. parents with kids 0–25, June 2021

Worry:
The act of mentally dwelling on outcomes beyond your control.

vast number of areas (at least all sixteen presented in this study) that parents feel may impact their kids' future and are likely somewhat out of a parent's control.

In the same way that parents place a high value on physical exercise and nutrition, parents rate good eating/nutrition (43.9%) and getting enough sleep (38.3%) as their top two causes of concern, saying they worry *often* or *all of the time* about these issues. This reinforces our understanding that parents place a significant priority on their kids' physical well-being.[10] By contrast, parents say they worry least about issues that may have been of greater concern to past generations— namely, drug use (19.4%), alcohol (15.2%), sexual behavior (16.9%), and faith (11.5%).

Anxiety:
A nebulous sense that something is wrong even though it's difficult to name specifically. Anxiety, unlike worry, often shows up in physiological symptoms like lightheadedness, nausea, or indigestion.

Parents also demonstrate substantial worry about their kids' mental health. More than a fourth (28%.3) of parents claim they worry *often* or *all the time* about anxiety, depression, body image, and suicide. These numbers may reflect the high value parents place on mental health (the top-scoring value in Section 1).

Levels of Worry

In contrast to the general population, parents who identify themselves as committed Christians worry substantially more about their kids' faith. More than 51% of Christian parents say they worry *often* or *all of the time* about their kids' faith compared to 11.5% of the general population of parents who say the same. Even more significant, however, is the degree to which Christian parents worry more about *every topic* listed in this study. Over twice as many Christian parents report feeling worried all of the time, as compared to the general population of parents. Plus, there was no topic listed about which Christian parents worried less than the general population of parents. <u>If Christian parents worry more than the average parent, then it may be worth asking: What is it about faith that intensifies levels of worry for Christian parents?</u> One might wonder if the level of worry is the natural outcome of adults who are more intentional in their caregiver responsibilities, or an indicator of underlying pressure to meet perceived standards? Perhaps it's neither or both, but ministry leaders who work with parents may want to take note of the heightened level of worry reported by parents in their church or parish.

What Parents Fear Most

→ Parents place a significant priority on their kids' physical well-being.

Despite the higher level of worry for Christian parents, all parents worry about the same things. Both the general parenting population and committed Christian parents consistently prioritize their areas of concern in a similar fashion. Three of the top five parenting worries are the same for Christian parents and the general population. And while Christian parents worry more about faith and peer influence than other parents, they share the general population's concern about bullies and anxiety, ranking them sixth and seventh, respectively, on their list.[11]

Section 02 — What Parents Fear — What Most Parents Aren't Telling You

Levels of Worry

How parents rate all 16 parenting concerns on average.

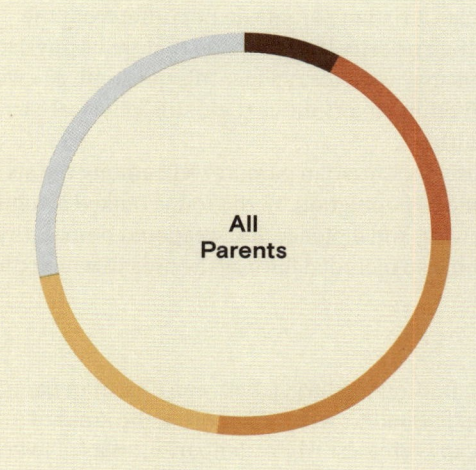

All Parents

8.6%	All of the Time
17.9%	Often
26.1%	Somewhat
19.6%	Rarely
28%	Not at All

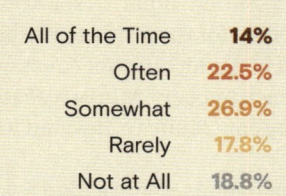

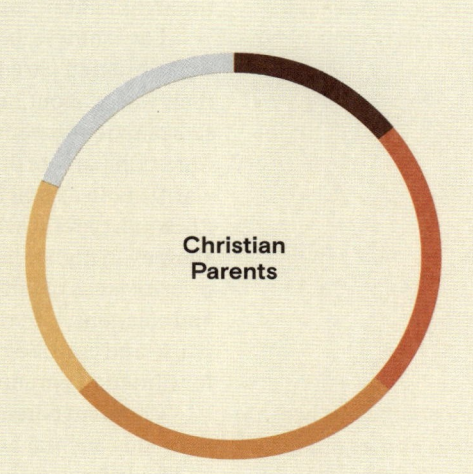

Christian Parents

All of the Time	**14%**
Often	**22.5%**
Somewhat	**26.9%**
Rarely	**17.8%**
Not at All	**18.8%**

n = 1,464 U.S. parents with kids 0–25, June 2021
n = 1,269 U.S. Christian parents with kids 0–25, February 2022

Section 02   What Parents Fear   What Most Parents Aren't Telling You

n = 1,464 U.S. parents with kids 0–25, June 2021

n = 1,269 U.S. Christian parents with kids 0–25, February 2022

All Parents' Top Five
#1 Good Eating/Nutrition
#2 Getting Enough Sleep
#3 Anxiousness
#4 Responsible Use of Technology
#5 Being Bullied by Other Kids

Christian Parents' Top Five
#1 Good Eating/Nutrition
#2 Getting Enough Sleep
#3 Influence of Peers
#4 Responsible Use of Technology
#5 Religious Faith

It's worth repeating that Christian parents do not differ from the general population in the high priority they place on their kids' physical well-being. Ministry leaders may wish to consider this question: Are we supporting parents in their efforts to prioritize their kids' physical—as well as their spiritual—health?

The lowest five concerns for Christian parents were among the six lowest concerns for the general population. Both groups ranked alcohol, drugs, suicide, sexual behavior, and violence and weapons comparatively low. The general population also included faith as the area in which they worry least for their kids.

Where the Gaps Widen

→ Nearly twice as many Christian parents report feeling worried all of the time, as compared to the general population of parents.

One of the more intriguing findings is the gap between Christian parents and the general population is smallest when comparing the areas of highest concern, and the gap is greatest when comparing areas of lowest concern. In other words, Christian parents worry substantially more in the areas of least concern to both groups.

For example, both sets of parents prioritize their kids' nutrition. And Christian parents differ from the general population of parents in their worry about nutrition by only a +2.7% margin. In contrast, both sets of parents spend less energy worrying about sexual behavior. And Christian parents differ from the general population of parents in their worry about sexual behavior by a greater than 13% margin. Moreover, Christian parents who attend church or parish services more frequently show even higher levels of worry for their kids in the otherwise low priority areas of faith, sexual behavior, alcohol consumption, violence and weapons, and the influence of peers. Ministry leaders may want to pause and consider what may contribute to elevated worry in these areas for Christian parents.

→ Three of the top five parenting worries are the same for Christian parents and the general population.

Christian parents, like all parents, share a high level of concern for their kids' mental health in the areas of anxiety, depression, suicide, and body image. As noted above, this high-concern bundle-of-worries is associated with a relatively small gap between the two groups. In contrast, Christian parents worry about their kids' relationships and physical health by a greater than 10% margin. The greatest difference between Christian parents and the general population of parents is the level of concern for their kids' faith. A little less than half (41%) of Christian parents say they worry *often* or *all the time* about their kid's faith, while the general population worries only 11.5% of the time in this area.

Section 02 — What Parents Fear — What Most Parents Aren't Telling You

Parents Differ Most in Their Low-Level Fears

The percent of parents who worry *often* or *all the time* about these concerns.

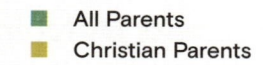

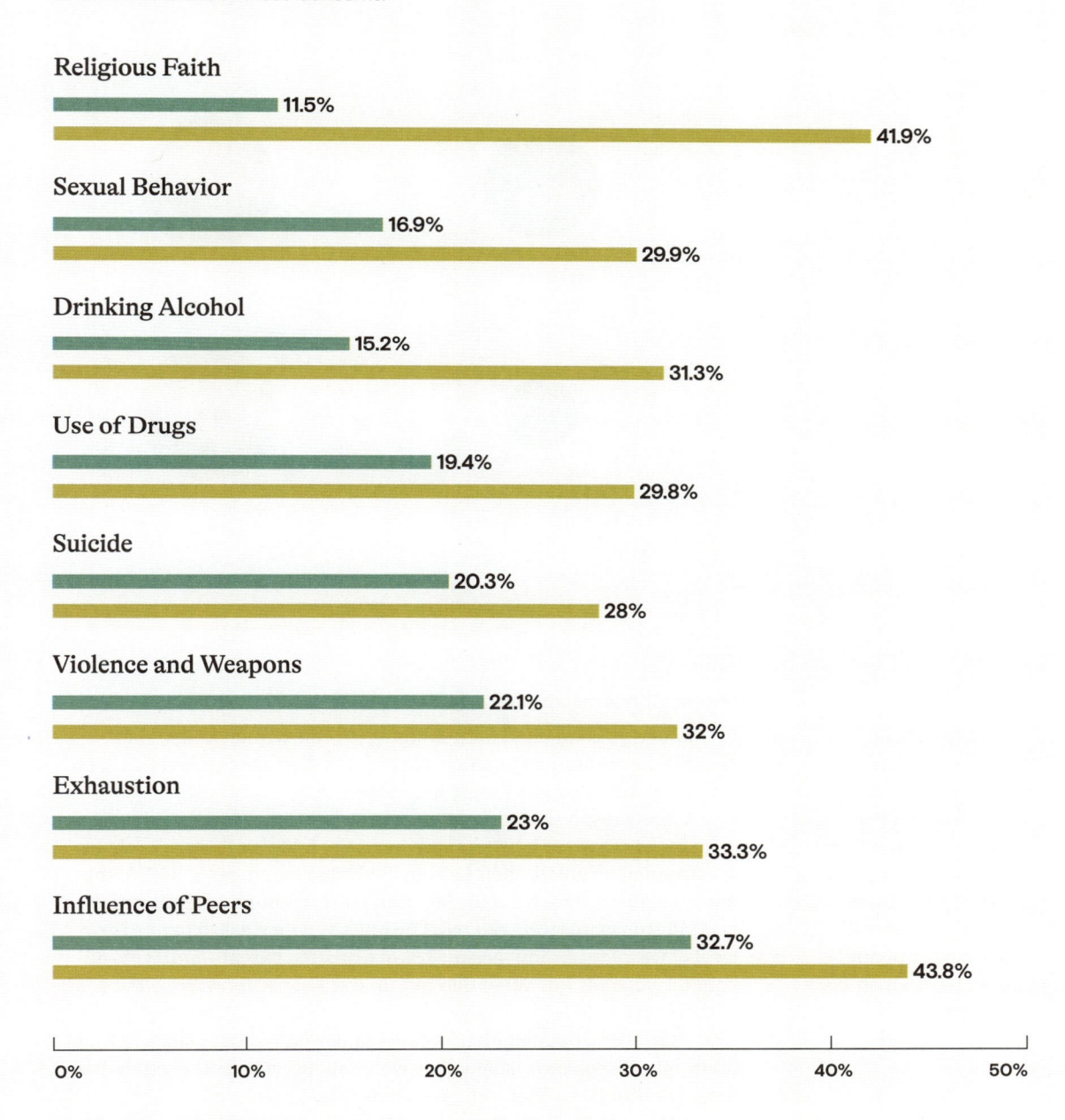

■ All Parents
■ Christian Parents

Religious Faith
- All Parents: 11.5%
- Christian Parents: 41.9%

Sexual Behavior
- All Parents: 16.9%
- Christian Parents: 29.9%

Drinking Alcohol
- All Parents: 15.2%
- Christian Parents: 31.3%

Use of Drugs
- All Parents: 19.4%
- Christian Parents: 29.8%

Suicide
- All Parents: 20.3%
- Christian Parents: 28%

Violence and Weapons
- All Parents: 22.1%
- Christian Parents: 32%

Exhaustion
- All Parents: 23%
- Christian Parents: 33.3%

Influence of Peers
- All Parents: 32.7%
- Christian Parents: 43.8%

n = 1,464 U.S. parents with kids 0–25, June 2021
n = 1,269 U.S. Christian parents with kids 0–25, February 2022

Parents Differ in Their Worry About Faith and Relationships

The percent of parents who worry about their kid's faith and relationships.

All Parents   **Christian Parents**

Relationships

(bullies, peers, sexual behavior, technology)

29.4%   39%

Faith

11.5%   41.9%

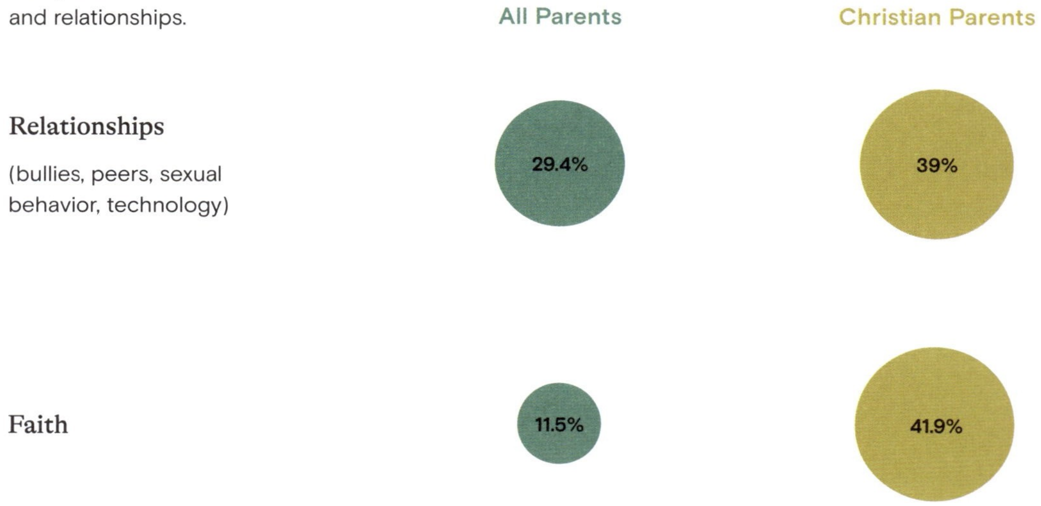

n = 1,464 U.S. parents with kids 0–25, June 2021
n = 1,269 U.S. Christian parents with kids 0–25, February 2022

→ Comparatively, Christian parents worry about mental health less often than they worry about their kid's relationships and physical health, while the general population worries more about mental health than any other issue.

Parent Concerns about Racism

In the surveys conducted for this study, parents demonstrated that racism was a prominent concern for them in their parenting, and that it was unlike other causes for parental worry.

Parents responded to an open-ended question, "What would you do to make the world a better place for your child?" with dreams about an imagined future for their kids. In analyzing parent responses to this question, racism stood out as the ninth most frequently mentioned word once all stop words were removed.[12] Similarly, when asked to rate their level of worry regarding racism, 31% of Christian parents and 23.6% of parents generally answered that racism was a cause for worry *often* or *all of the time*.

The general population of parents rank worry about racism as their tenth-highest concern, saying they worry about racism more often than faith, sex, drugs, alcohol, violence, or suicide.

While this study did not explore the full scope of what participants meant by these responses, one might wonder if parental fear about the impact of racism is associated with other parenting values and concerns. Are parents who worry about racism worried about how racism might impact their kid's access to resources, education, careers, and opportunities? Are parents who worry about racism worried about how racism might impact their kid's mental and physical health? Are parents who worry about racism worried about how racism might impact their kid's relationships, or expose their kids to violence? These questions provide direction for further exploration in order to better understand how to interpret parent responses in this area.[13]

One particular characteristic of racism is that it does not impact all parents equally. Unsurprisingly, this study found parents worry about the impact of racism on their kids differently according to their own racial or ethnic identity. Parents who are White worry about racism least (17%), followed by Asian parents (25%) then Hispanic and Latino parents (32%). Nearly half (45%) of Black and African-American parents worry about racism *often* or *all of the time*.

Parents who worry about racism may be looking for resources to help them raise kids who are capable of recognizing and navigating racial bias. Additionally, parents who worry about racism may hope to see an acknowledgment of racism in parenting literature holistically, given the potential for racism to impact other parenting values and fears.

Parents Differ in Their Concerns About Racism

For every two White parents who worry about racism, three Asian parents, four Latino parents, and six Black parents worry about racism.

→ For more information about our race and income demographics, see our Notes on page 125.

n = 1,464 U.S. parents with kids 0–25, June 2021

Section 02 — What Parents Fear — What Most Parents Aren't Telling You

Christian Parent Concerns About Church

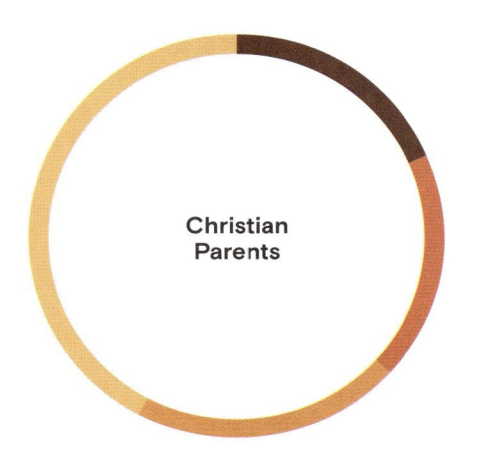

Survey Statement
I have concerns about what my faith community teaches my kids.

18.4% Very True
18.4% Moderately True
21% Mildly True
42.1% Untrue

Survey Statement
I have concerns about how my faith community welcomes/accommodates my kids.

20.1% Very True
18.8% Moderately True
19.8% Mildly True
41.3% Untrue

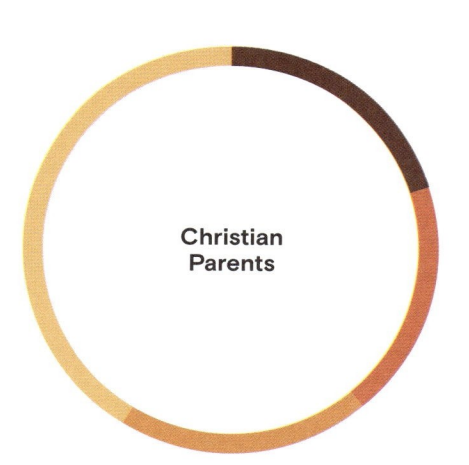

n = 1,269 U.S. Christian parents with kids 0–25, February 2022

Parent Concerns About Faith & Church

Christian parents place a high value on the faith of their kids, but this level of enthusiasm comes with significantly elevated levels of worry. Seventy percent of Christian parents say they worry *somewhat, often,* or *all of the time* about their kids' faith compared to only 30% who say they worry *rarely* or *never* in this area. In fact, Christian parents rank faith as their fifth-highest worry, just after technology, peers, sleep, and nutrition.

In addition to worrying about their kids' faith, Christian parents also indicate levels of concern about their kids experience at church. Over half of committed Christian parents have some level of concern about what their church or parish teaches and how their church or parish welcomes their kids.

When it comes to the content that faith communities teach preschoolers, elementary kids, middle schoolers, high schoolers, and young adults, what are parents worried about? We can't say conclusively. Parents express consistent and moderate concern about the developmental appropriateness, Biblical or theological accuracy, and future impact of content on their kids—between 32% and 38%, indicating concern in all three areas *often* or *all of the time*. Similarly, when asked what parents would like to see their church teach *more of* or *less of*, parents are divided in their responses. Between 30% and 40% of parents indicate a desire for more *and* a desire for less of every teaching, without any general consensus.[14] Ministry leaders may frequently find themselves caught between those who want more and those who want less of any given teaching.

However, the most likely indicator of what parents are worried about—the 58% of Christian parents who say they have some level of worry about what their church or parish teaches their kids—may be found in parent responses concerning specific, and somewhat divisive, topics. When asked whether they agree or disagree with the statement, "I worry that my church teaches differently than me" on a series of topics, Christian parents responded with a strong affirmative. Almost half of all parents have concerns that their church or parish teaches differently from them on some issues including: LGBTQIA (55%), self-worth (48.1%), creation (47.9%), the Bible (46.7%), and salvation (45.7%). These findings may be a reminder to astute leaders that a significant portion of committed Christian parents are aware of their role in these conversations, and may worry about what others say to their kids on these topics.

One of the survey respondents put her concerns this way, "I just don't know what some people teach my kid while I'm in church." If this is a common sentiment, it may be that some parents would like more transparent and preemptive communication about how leaders will teach or present on certain issues.

> Almost half of all parents have concerns that their church or parish teaches differently from them on some issues.

> Parental concern for bullying peaks as soon as a kid enters school (4–5 years old) and remains constant through the beginning of high school.

In addition to content concerns, parents responded with similar levels of worry about how their faith community welcomes their kids, with 58.7% of Christian parents claiming they have some level of concern in this area. In order to better understand these concerns, we asked parents to respond to an open-ended question: "How could your faith community be more welcoming to your kids?" The responses generally fell into one of five categories with a few outliers.

While ministry leaders may find Christian parents' concerns about their church's ability to instruct and welcome their kids challenging, there are a few encouraging takeaways to keep in mind. Christian parents are less worried about what their faith community teaches or how their faith community welcomes their kids than they are about their kids faith generally. And Christian parents also worry less about what their faith community teaches or how their faith community welcomes their kids than they worry about any other parenting concern listed in this study. We also found encouraging results in the level of support parents feel when connected to a faith community, which we will discuss in section 3.

Section 02 · What Parents Fear · What Most Parents Aren't Telling You

59% of Christian Parents Worry About How Their Faith Community Welcomes & Accommodates Their Kid

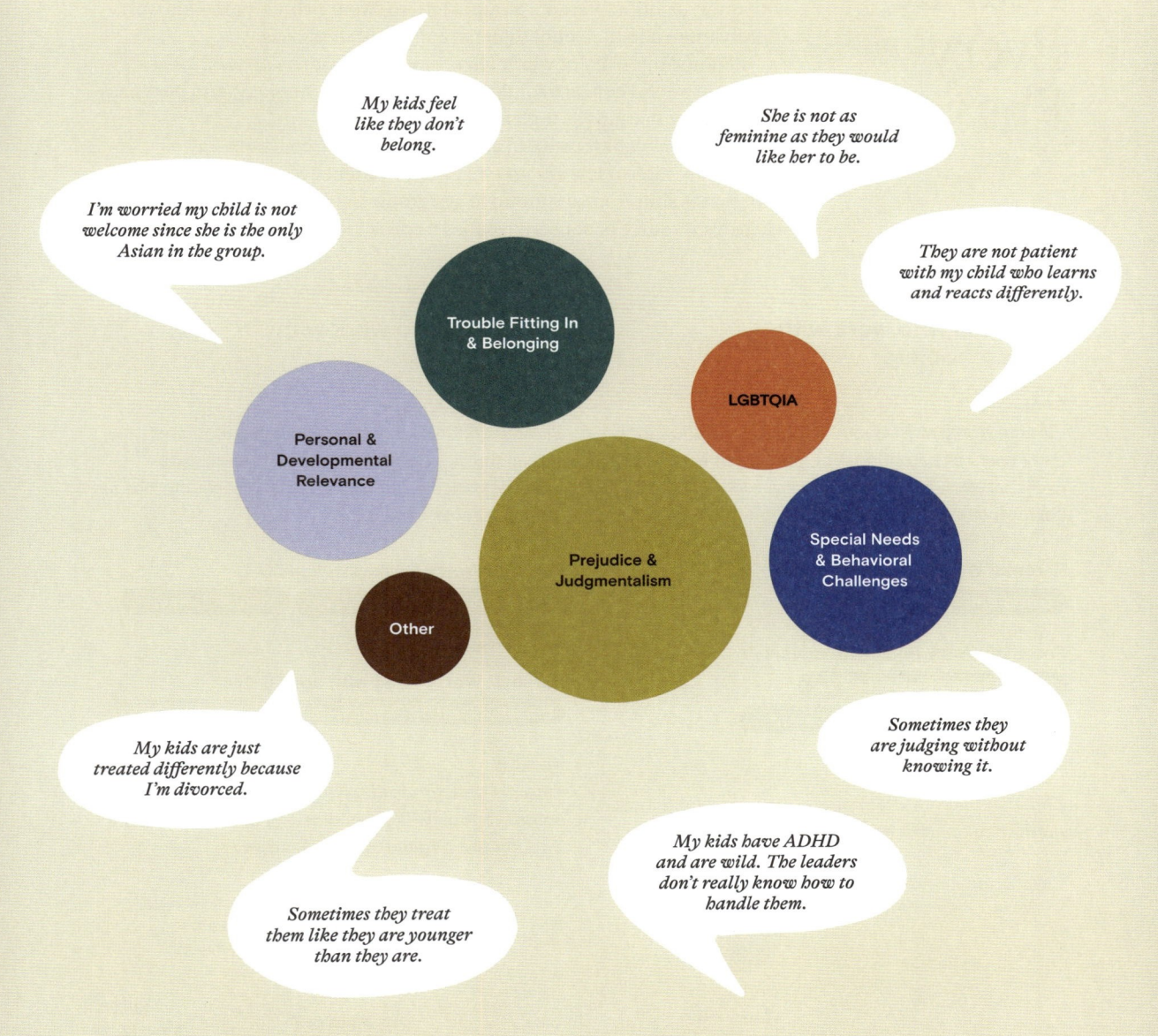

I'm worried my child is not welcome since she is the only Asian in the group.

My kids feel like they don't belong.

She is not as feminine as they would like her to be.

They are not patient with my child who learns and reacts differently.

Trouble Fitting In & Belonging

Personal & Developmental Relevance

LGBTQIA

Prejudice & Judgmentalism

Special Needs & Behavioral Challenges

Other

My kids are just treated differently because I'm divorced.

Sometimes they treat them like they are younger than they are.

Sometimes they are judging without knowing it.

My kids have ADHD and are wild. The leaders don't really know how to handle them.

n = 847 U.S. Christian parents with kids 0–25, March 2022

Section 02   What Parents Fear   What Most Parents Aren't Telling You

What Parents Fear at Every Phase

As a child moves through the phases, parents differ more in their fears than they do in their values.

Only good eating/nutrition remains a top-three concern at almost every phase, but it did not claim the top spot for parents of middle and high school age kids, as new worries escalate in those phases. The lowest three worries consistently remain faith, sexual behavior, and alcohol with one exception. Parents of nineteen- to twenty-three-year-olds worry slightly more about alcohol than parents in other phases.

Parents' intensity of worry also changes across the phases. Most notably, parental concern for depression, use of technology, and busyness fluctuates by margins as high as 20%.

While the highest concern and the lowest three concerns stay consistently high or low across every phase, parents' level of worry for each source does shift from age group to age group. Below, we highlight the phase where each source of concern reaches its peak level of reported worry.

For those who work with
→ **Preschoolers**

Summary
Parents worry most about sleep and nutrition in the early years of parenting. But, parents of four- and five-year-olds also worry about anxiety in their children as often as they worry about sleep.

Parental Worry Peak with ages 0-3
- Good Eating/Nutrition

Parental Worry Peak with ages 4-5
- Being Bullied by Other Kids
- Religious Faith (Christian Parents)

Notable
Christian parents worry about their kids' faith most when they are four and five years old.

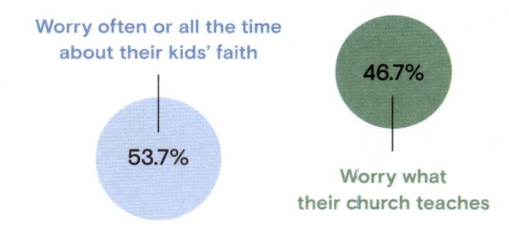

- 53.7% Worry often or all the time about their kids' faith
- 46.7% Worry what their church teaches

n = 1,269 U.S. Christian parents with kids 0–25, February 2022

For those who work with
→ **Elementary**

Summary
Parents continue to worry about nutrition and bullies throughout the elementary years. And, parental concern for a kid's anxiety begins to rise in the late preteen years.[15]

Parental Worry Peak with ages 6-7
- Being Bullied by Other Kids
- Sexual Behavior
- Use of Technology

Parental Worry Peak with ages 8-11
- Being Bullied by Other Kids
- Influence of Peers

Notable
Parental concern for bullying peaks as soon as a kid enters school (6-7 years old) and remains constant through the beginning of high school.

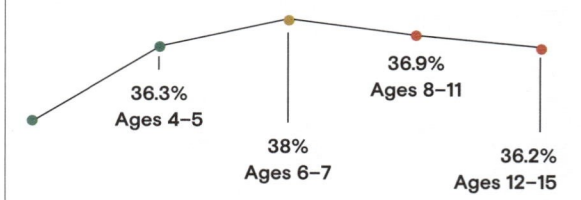

- 36.3% Ages 4–5
- 38% Ages 6–7
- 36.9% Ages 8–11
- 36.2% Ages 12–15

Percentage of parents who worry *often* or *all the time* about their kid being bullied by other kids.

Section 02 — What Parents Fear — What Most Parents Aren't Telling You

For those who work with
→ **Middle Schoolers**

Summary
Parents worry increasingly more about their kids' anxiety, depression, suicide, body image, busyness and exhaustion as their kids enter this phase.

Parental Worry Peak with ages 12–15
- Being Bullied by Other Kids
- Sexual Behavior
- Getting Enough Sleep

Notable
Parents worry about their kids' sleep during the middle school years more than at any other phase.

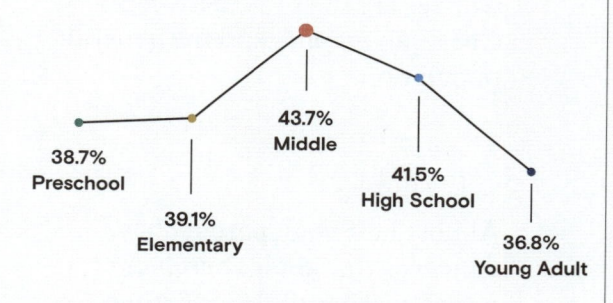

- 38.7% Preschool
- 39.1% Elementary
- 43.7% Middle
- 41.5% High School
- 36.8% Young Adult

Values are percentages of parents who worry *often* or *all the time* about their kid getting enough sleep.

For those who work with
→ **High Schoolers**

Summary
The greatest number of parental concerns peak during the high school years.

Parental Worry Peak with ages 16–18
- Anxiety
- Depression
- Use of Drugs
- Alcohol
- Suicide
- Racism

Notable
The greatest number of fears peak during this phase, but they aren't all equal.

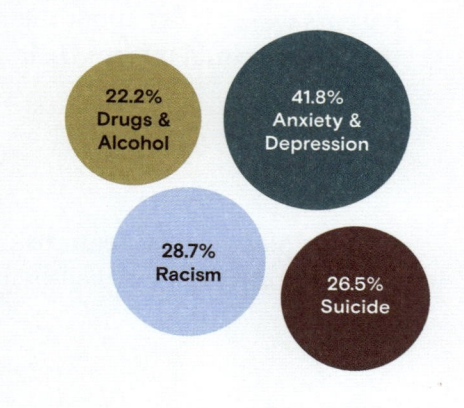

- 22.2% Drugs & Alcohol
- 41.8% Anxiety & Depression
- 28.7% Racism
- 26.5% Suicide

For those who work with
→ **Young Adults**

Notable
The general population reports higher levels of worry about faith when their kid is nineteen to twenty-five years old.

10.3%
Worry about their kids faith

Christian parents report having their highest level of concern about how their faith community welcomes their kid during the young adult phase.

55.4%
Worry how their church welcomes their kid

Parental Worry Peak with ages 23–25
- Violence and Weapons
- Body Image
- Busyness/Exhaustion

---

n = 1,464 U.S. parents with kids 0–25, June 2021   n = 1,269 U.S. Christian parents with kids 0–25, February 2022

Key Findings: What Parents Fear

01
Parents worry most about the things that could impact their kids' future.

02
Parents place a significant priority on their kids' physical well-being.

03
Nearly twice as many Christian parents report feeling worried *all of the time*, as compared to the general population of parents.

04
Three of the top five parenting worries are the same between Christian parents and the general population.

05
Almost half of all parents have concerns that their church or parish teaches differently than them on some issues.

06
Parental concern for bullying peaks as soon as a kid enters school (4-5yrs) and remains constant through the beginning of high school.

07

As a child moves from birth, through preschool, elementary, middle and high school, and into their young adult years, parents differ more in their fears and worries than they do in their values.

08

Parents' top three and bottom five values remain constant across the phases, but parenting worries shift more from phase to phase.

09

White parents worry about racism least (17%), followed by Asian parents (25%), then Hispanic and Latino parents (32%). Nearly half (46%) of Black and African-American parents worry about racism *often* or *all of the time*.

10

For every two White parents who worry about racism, three Asian parents, four Latino parents, and six Black parents worry about racism.

If you don't have a
secret stash of all the
good snacks hidden
somewhere, are you
even a parent?

Section #03

HOW PARENTS FEEL

→ Anyone raising young people will tell you, parenting is no easy task. Parents care about their kids' future and place a high value on everything from healthy mentors to education to physical exercise for their kids. In an unpredictable world filled with challenges and risks, parents also tend to worry about the things that might sabotage their kids' future. When you add the values and worries of parenting together with the generous amount of love most parents feel for the young person they are raising, it all comes to quite a sum of emotions. Maybe the real question is: How do parents feel?

Parents are people too, after all. Caring for the holistic needs of another person can feel overwhelming and costly. Furthermore, a surprising amount of research demonstrates that for many, the benefits of parenting do not outweigh the mental and emotional toll. Parents overall demonstrate a lower level of emotional well-being than non-parents, and possibly moreso in the United States.[16] Ministry leaders who care about the future of young people should take note of this parenting paradox. Nothing may influence a kid more than the mental, social, emotional, and spiritual health of their parent. At the same time, the act of parenting itself may negatively impact a parent's mental and emotional health.

To further compound this paradox, the way a parent feels about their parenting impacts a parent's ability to successfully meet the needs of their kids. Research in psychology and sociology both pursue this topic with such deliberation there's a term for it: *parenting self-efficacy* or *PSE* for short.[17]

Parenting self-efficacy describes a parent's belief in their ability to perform the parenting role effectively. And higher levels of PSE have been associated with a wide range of positive parent and child outcomes.[18] Generally speaking, the more a parent believes in their own ability to parent their child, the more likely they are to provide an adaptive, stimulating, and nurturing environment that encourages social, academic, and psychological well-being.[19] Simply put: When parents feel good about their ability to parent, everyone wins.

Section 03 How Parents Feel What Most Parents Aren't Telling You

How Parents Feel About Themselves as Parents

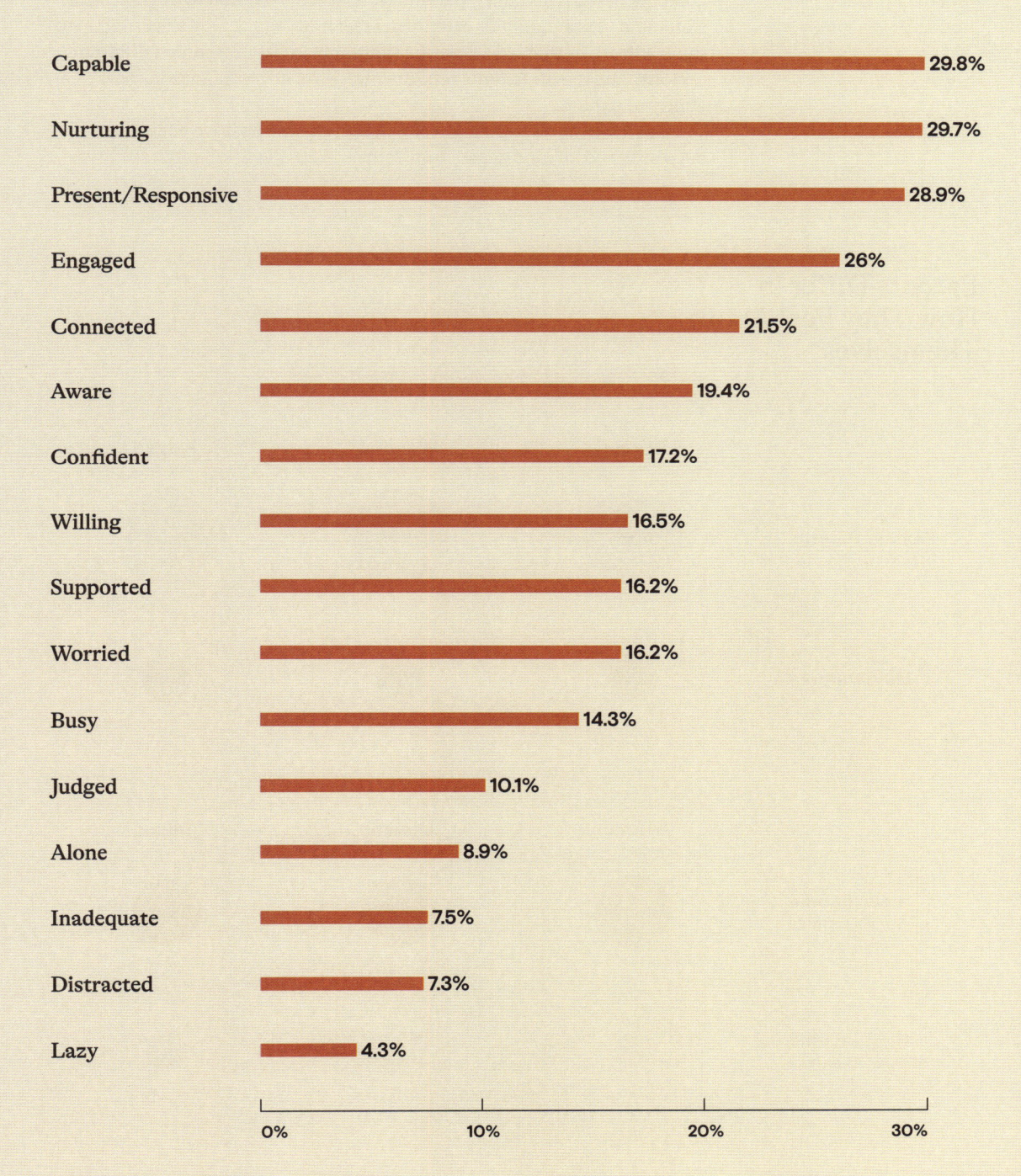

Trait	Percentage
Capable	29.8%
Nurturing	29.7%
Present/Responsive	28.9%
Engaged	26%
Connected	21.5%
Aware	19.4%
Confident	17.2%
Willing	16.5%
Supported	16.2%
Worried	16.2%
Busy	14.3%
Judged	10.1%
Alone	8.9%
Inadequate	7.5%
Distracted	7.3%
Lazy	4.3%

n = 1,464 U.S. parents with kids 0–25, June 2021

Section 03   How Parents Feel   What Most Parents Aren't Telling You

Human Parent Feelings

→ Parents report a high level of confidence in their ability to parent.

So, how do parents feel about their ability to parent? In general, pretty good. As part of this study, parents were asked to complete the following statement. "As a parent or caregiver, I feel that I am . . ." by selecting up to three adjectives that best describe them from a list of eighteen different options. The result: Parents report a high level of confidence in their ability to parent.

For the general population of parents, all nine positive adjectives outperformed all nine negative adjectives. A 2015 Pew Research study on

Parents Differ in How They Feel About Themselves

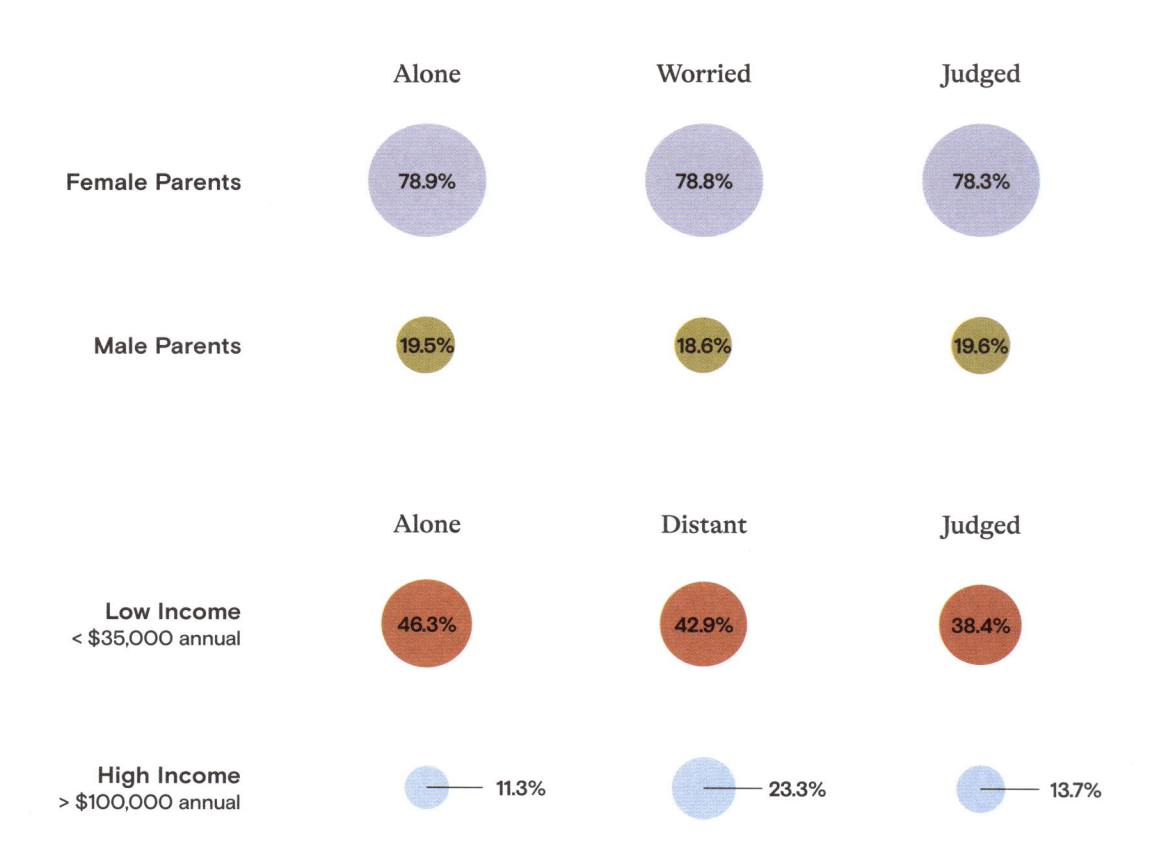

	Alone	Worried	Judged
Female Parents	78.9%	78.8%	78.3%
Male Parents	19.5%	18.6%	19.6%

	Alone	Distant	Judged
Low Income < $35,000 annual	46.3%	42.9%	38.4%
High Income > $100,000 annual	11.3%	23.3%	13.7%

n = 1,464 U.S. parents with kids 0–25, June 2021

Parenting in America revealed similar findings. Pew reported that nearly half (45%) of all parents said they are doing a *very good* job, and similar shares said they were doing a *good* job of parenting their kids.[20] Millennial parents were even more likely to give themselves high marks. Leaders who communicate with parents may want to consider this: How does parenting confidence impact the way we communicate with parents?

Before jumping to too many conclusions, it's important to note two variables that significantly impact this picture: gender and income. Unlike the general combined responses, female parents selected *alone* (78.9%), *worried* (78.8%), and *judged* (78.3%) more than any other adjective on the list. Conversely, male parents selected these three adjectives least often, but 54% of male parents selected *confused*. This suggests that while parents feel generally positive about their parenting, other emotions are still at play. Moreover, income is likely to impact the way a parent feels. Parents with an annual family income of $35,000 or less selected *alone* (46.3%), *distant* (42.9%), and *judged* (38.4%) more than any other adjective on the list. One might imagine how the impacts of both gender and income can be compounding for some parents.

Parents also report a high level of confidence in their ability to understand their kids. Compared to other adults in their kids' life, 61.2% of all parents say they know their kids *more than other adults do*. And 26% of parents say other adults *frequently don't understand their kids*. The gap between how a parent understands their kids and how a parent perceives other adults' understanding of their kids highlights a potential source of frustration for some parents. Parents may find themselves tasked with advocating on behalf of their kids in numerous arenas—from education, to health, to resources. Female parents rate themselves more highly on their ability to understand their kids, which may mean they feel a disproportionate burden to help other adults understand their kids more completely.

What Parents Feel Most

Faith has little impact on the way parents report feeling about their parenting with one exception. Christian parents did not differ from the general population in their level of overall positivity. For Christian parents, as with the general population, all nine positive adjectives outperformed all nine negative adjectives. And, both groups rated four of the same adjectives in their top five, saying they feel *capable*, *nurturing*, *engaged*, and *connected*.

Christian parents also did not differ from the general population in their top three negative descriptors. Both groups of parents rated the same three negative adjectives highest behind all positive options, saying they often feel *worried*, *busy*, and *judged*. Similar to the general population, both income and gender impacted Christian parents' perception of their parenting.

→ **Top Three Negative**
#1 Worried
#2 Busy
#3 Judged

n = 1,464 U.S. parents with kids 0–25, June 2021

n = 1,269 U.S. Christian parents with kids 0–25, February 2022

All Parents' Top Five
#1 Capable
#2 Nurturing
#3 Present/Responsive
#4 Engaged
#5 Connected

Christian Parents' Top Five
#1 Connected
#2 Capable
#3 Nurturing
#4 Supported
#5 Engaged

Where the Gaps Widen

In contrast to all parents, 27.3% of Christian parents selected *supported* as a top three adjective to describe their parenting. Only 18.2% of the general parent population selected this adjective. Moreover, Christian parents who attend church or parish services more frequently say they feel *supported* more often and *alone* less often than Christian parents who attend services less frequently.

Christian parents also have a higher perception of the other adult influences in their kids' life. Christian parents do not differ from the general population in feeling that they understand more about their kids than other adults. But, 33.2% of Christian parents, compared to 20.5% of the general parenting population, say other adults know their child very well. While these findings are encouraging, they cannot confirm the specific source of this 14% increase in confidence. One might hope it's a reflection that churches and parishes are successfully training volunteers and adults within the faith community to better understand the needs of kids and teenagers.

How Well Parents Think Other Adults Know Their Kids

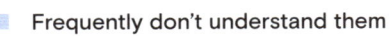

- Frequently don't understand them
- Understand them well enough
- Understand them very well

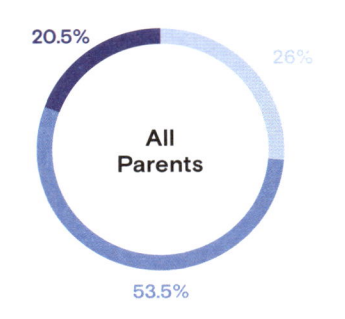

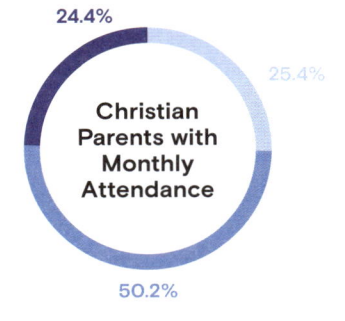

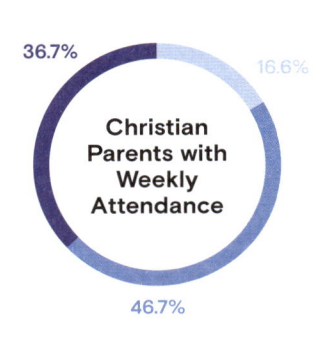

All Parents
- 20.5%
- 26%
- 53.5%

Christian Parents with Monthly Attendance
- 24.4%
- 25.4%
- 50.2%

Christian Parents with Weekly Attendance
- 36.7%
- 16.6%
- 46.7%

n = 1,464 U.S. parents with kids 0–25, June 2021
n = 1,269 U.S. Christian parents with kids 0–25, February 2022

Section 03 How Parents Feel What Most Parents Aren't Telling You

How Parents Feel Supported

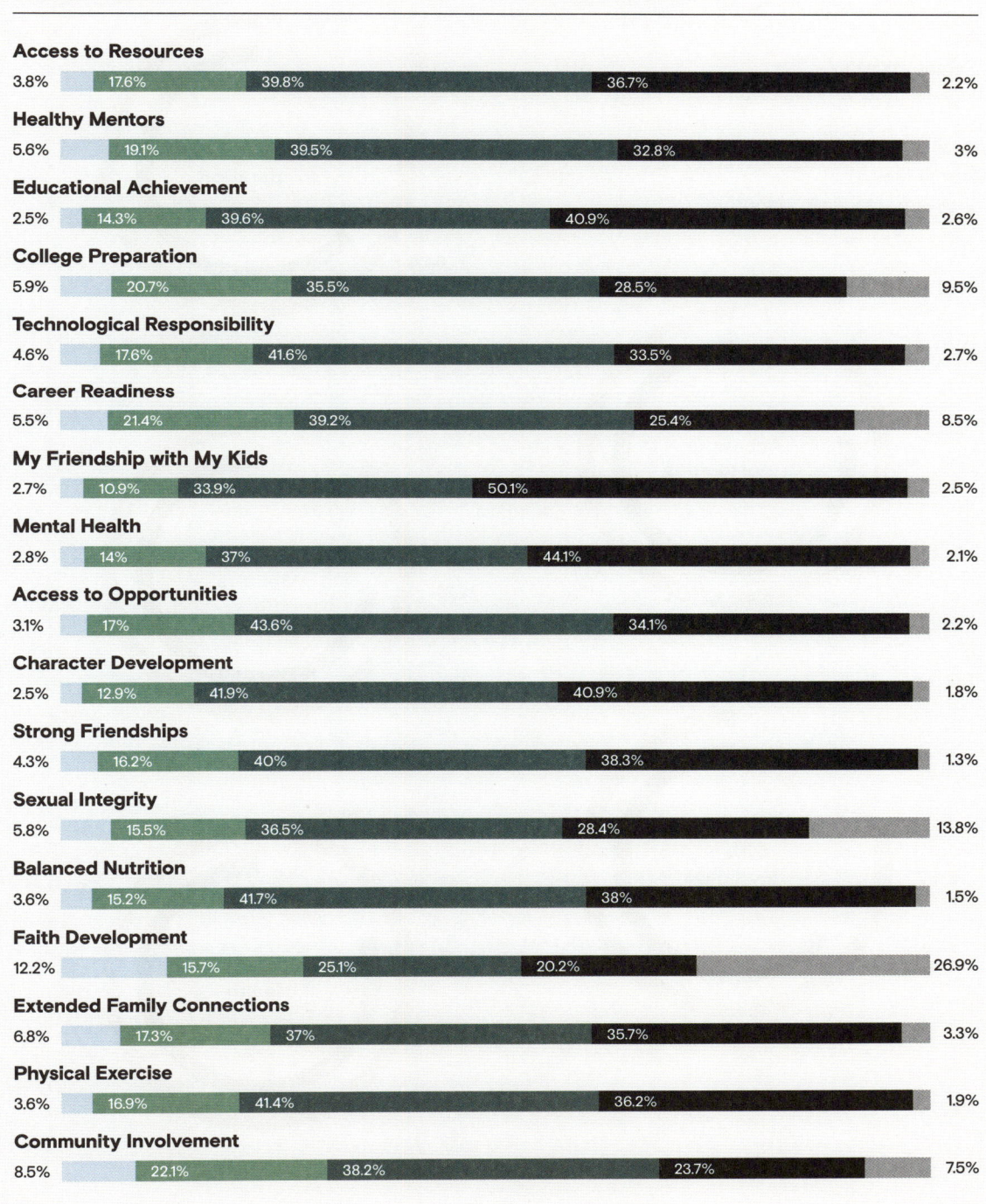

Legend: Unsupported | Somewhat Supported | Supported | Well-Supported | Not Applicable

Access to Resources
3.8% | 17.6% | 39.8% | 36.7% | 2.2%

Healthy Mentors
5.6% | 19.1% | 39.5% | 32.8% | 3%

Educational Achievement
2.5% | 14.3% | 39.6% | 40.9% | 2.6%

College Preparation
5.9% | 20.7% | 35.5% | 28.5% | 9.5%

Technological Responsibility
4.6% | 17.6% | 41.6% | 33.5% | 2.7%

Career Readiness
5.5% | 21.4% | 39.2% | 25.4% | 8.5%

My Friendship with My Kids
2.7% | 10.9% | 33.9% | 50.1% | 2.5%

Mental Health
2.8% | 14% | 37% | 44.1% | 2.1%

Access to Opportunities
3.1% | 17% | 43.6% | 34.1% | 2.2%

Character Development
2.5% | 12.9% | 41.9% | 40.9% | 1.8%

Strong Friendships
4.3% | 16.2% | 40% | 38.3% | 1.3%

Sexual Integrity
5.8% | 15.5% | 36.5% | 28.4% | 13.8%

Balanced Nutrition
3.6% | 15.2% | 41.7% | 38% | 1.5%

Faith Development
12.2% | 15.7% | 25.1% | 20.2% | 26.9%

Extended Family Connections
6.8% | 17.3% | 37% | 35.7% | 3.3%

Physical Exercise
3.6% | 16.9% | 41.4% | 36.2% | 1.9%

Community Involvement
8.5% | 22.1% | 38.2% | 23.7% | 7.5%

n = 1,464 U.S. parents with kids 0–25, June 2021

Section 03   How Parents Feel   What Most Parents Aren't Telling You

The Gap Between Parent Values and Support

■ Parent values as *Important* to *Very Important*

■ Parent feels *Supported* to *Very Supported*

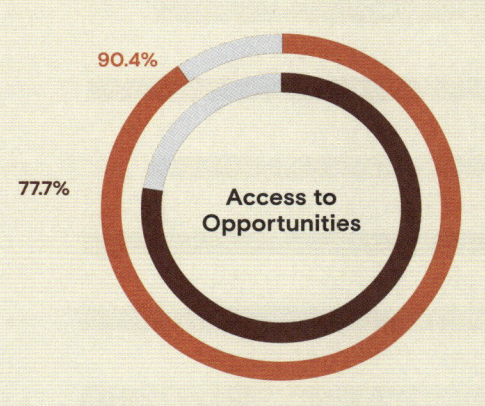

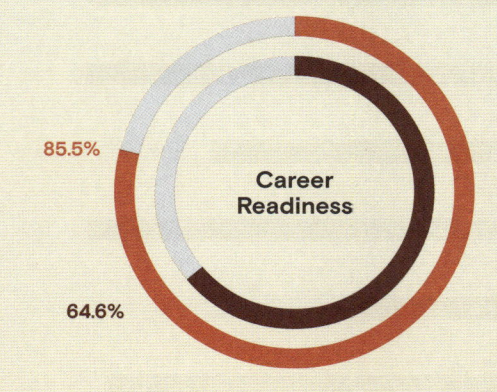

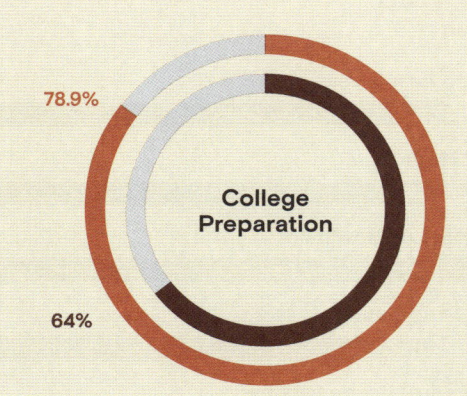

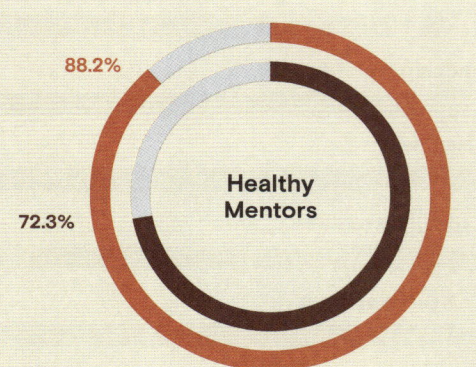

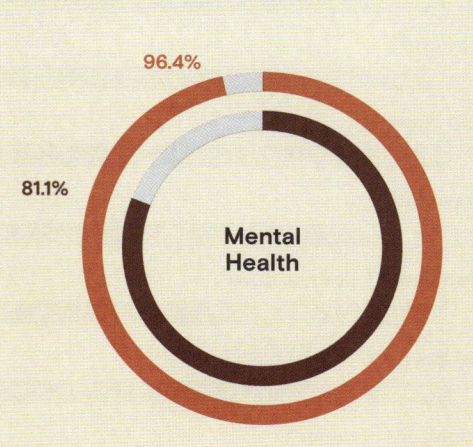

College Preparation
78.9%
64%

Access to Opportunities
90.4%
77.7%

Healthy Mentors
88.2%
72.3%

Career Readiness
85.5%
64.6%

Mental Health
96.4%
81.1%

n = 1,464 U.S. parents with kids 0–25, June 2021

How Human Parents Feel Supported

A large majority of parents may not have selected supported as one of the top three adjectives to describe themselves, but does that mean parents don't feel supported? Or, maybe a better question is: How supported do parents feel? In general, more than one might think.

When asked to rate their level of support in a number of parenting areas, on average, more parents in the general population say they feel *supported* to *well-supported* (72.8%) as opposed to only *somewhat* or *unsupported* (21.6%) in these areas. The remaining 6% of parents claim support was *not applicable* in the areas listed. While this is good news on the whole, one in twenty parents still report feeling fully unsupported in their parenting. And not every parent feels sufficiently supported in every area.

Unsurprisingly, the general population feels least supported in their kids' faith development. A full 12% feel unsupported, and 26.9% feel support in this area is *not applicable*. Given that 41.3% of the general parent population say their kids' faith is *unimportant* or *not applicable*, the value-to-support gap may not be all that wide. Following faith, the next lowest areas of support for parents are the following: community involvement (30.6%), career readiness (26.9%), and college preparation (26.6%).

Although parents were not asked to directly compare parenting values against levels of support for this study, the comparative findings may be instructive. Of the areas parents rated highest in importance (top three), parents report the lowest level of support in access to opportunities. Ministry leaders may want to consider asking parents in their community more about the kind of opportunities they want for their kids. Why are parents seeking these opportunities? What do they hope to gain for their kids? And how might ministries support parents by discovering what's already available, and connecting parents to the kind of opportunities they are looking for?

Parents also seem to indicate a gap between value and support in the areas of career readiness, healthy mentors, college preparation, and mental health. Again, the question seems to be: How might ministries re-imagine support for parents in the areas parents indicate needing it most?

The most notable finding related to parental support was the impact of income.[21] Parents with lower income report feeling less supported for thirteen of seventeen areas of parenting. In fact, the only areas where income did not impact perceived levels of support were friendship with my kids, mental health, strong friendships, and faith development. This vast economic disparity in parental support raises a number of questions: Who will provide support for low-income parents? Will ministry leaders step into the gap? If so, what low-income parent-support systems have a track record of efficacy? Where are the healthy models?

→ Parents with lower income report feeling less supported for thirteen of seventeen areas of parenting.

→ Those who attend faith services almost every week report higher levels of support than those who attend less frequently.

Levels of Support

How supported parents feel in 17 parenting values on average.

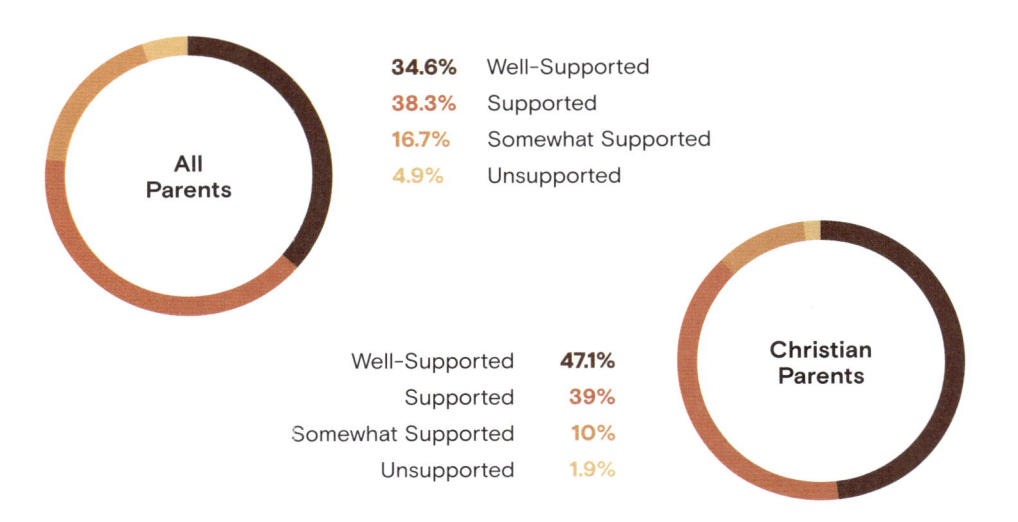

All Parents

- **34.6%** Well-Supported
- **38.3%** Supported
- **16.7%** Somewhat Supported
- **4.9%** Unsupported

Christian Parents

- Well-Supported **47.1%**
- Supported **39%**
- Somewhat Supported **10%**
- Unsupported **1.9%**

n = 1,464 U.S. parents with kids 0–25, June 2021
n = 1,269 U.S. Christian parents with kids 0–25, February 2022

→ Christian parents feel more positive about how their church influences their kids' future than they feel about how their church influences their parenting.

Levels of Support

Some leaders may wonder, "Is it possible or practical for ministries to support parents in all these ways in addition to creating quality experiences and relational networks for kids and teenagers?" The answer seems to be an overwhelming, "Yes, and . . ." Churches are already getting a few things right in this area. Almost half (47.1%) of Christian parents, compared to 31.4% of the general population, feel *well-supported* in their parenting overall.

Nowhere is the difference in support more noticeable than in the area of faith. Twice as many Christian parents, as compared to all parents, report feeling *supported* or *well-supported* in their kids' faith development.[22] But, faith isn't the only noticeable difference. Christian parents also report feeling significantly more supported in their kids' career readiness, college preparation, community involvement, extended family connections, sexual integrity, and healthy mentors.

Christian parents did not differ from the general population in the level of support they feel for two of the most highly valued areas of parenting: mental health and character development. This lack of

Section 03 How Parents Feel What Most Parents Aren't Telling You

Parents Differ in Key Areas of Support

■ All Parents
■ Christian Parents

Extended Family
- All Parents: 72.6%
- Christian Parents: 86%

Health Mentors
- All Parents: 72.3%
- Christian Parents: 85%

Career Readiness
- All Parents: 64.6%
- Christian Parents: 83%

Sexual Integrity
- All Parents: 64.9%
- Christian Parents: 83%

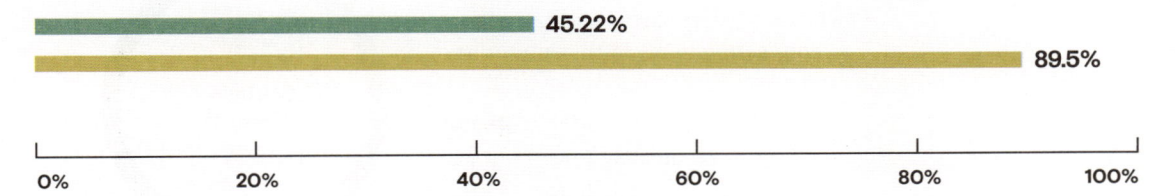

College Prep
- All Parents: 64%
- Christian Parents: 80%

Health
- All Parents: 76.6%
- Christian Parents: 87.9%

Faith
- All Parents: 45.22%
- Christian Parents: 89.5%

0%   20%   40%   60%   80%   100%

n = 1,464 U.S. parents with kids 0–25, June 2021
n = 1,269 U.S. Christian parents with kids 0–25, February 2022

difference may further emphasize a desire for more support in both areas, especially for Christian parents.

Christian parents, like all parents, say they feel least supported in the areas of community involvement, career readiness, and college preparation. Christian parents do, however, report feeling more supported than all parents for these otherwise low-support areas, which means Christian parents feel a more consistent level of parenting support overall. (The lows aren't as low.)

Church participation also makes a difference. Those who attend faith services almost every week report higher levels of support than those who attend less frequently. In light of these findings, one might wonder: Is there a connection between faith generally and a parent feeling supported? If faith communities are providing a positive context for parental support, what specifically are churches doing right in this area? How might a church or parish continue to measure parental support as a metric for overall ministry success?

The Church's Impact on Parents' Feelings

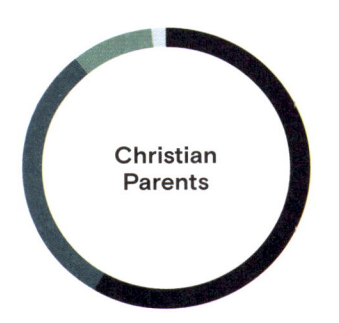

Christian Parents

Survey Statement
I feel more positive and optimistic about my kid's future because of our involvement in the faith community.

58.5% Very True
30.7% Moderately True
9.4% Mildly True
1.4% Untrue

Survey Statement
I feel I am a better parent because of my connection to my faith community.

Very True **46.1%**
Moderately True **31.1%**
Mildly True **17%**
Untrue 5.8%

Christian Parents

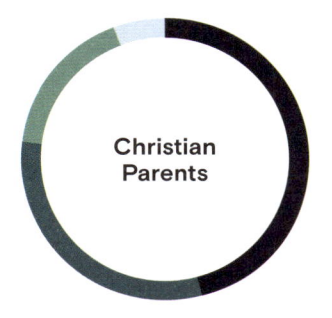

n = 1,269 U.S. Christian parents with kids 0–25, February 2022

Opportunities for Empathy and Understanding

Survey Statement
My faith community could be more supportive if they understood more about…

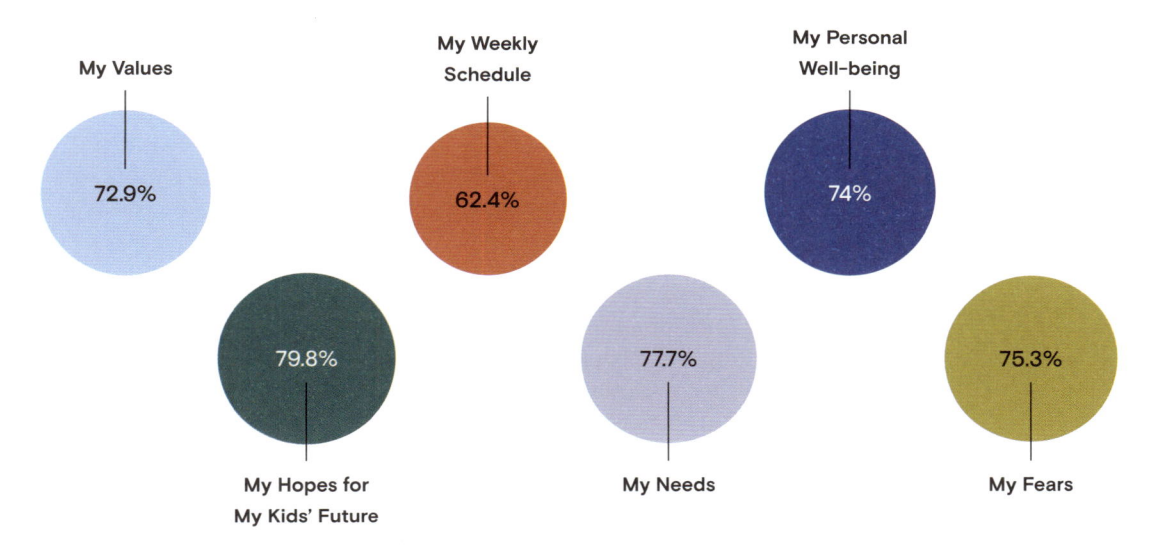

- My Values — 72.9%
- My Weekly Schedule — 62.4%
- My Personal Well-being — 74%
- My Hopes for My Kids' Future — 79.8%
- My Needs — 77.7%
- My Fears — 75.3%

n = 847 U.S. Christian parents with kids 0–25, March 2022

How Parents Feel Supported by the Church

Christian parents feel overall more supported than all parents. But, are Christian parents aware of how their involvement in a faith community impacts their level of support? And, how do Christian parents say they feel when asked directly about the level of support they receive from their church?

Here's where the findings become a little more complex. Christian parents feel more positive about how their church influences their kids' future than they feel about how their church influences their parenting. Christian parents were asked to respond separately to two questions probing the impact of church involvement on their parenting and on their kids' future. Compared to 89% of Christian parents who feel their church involvement has a substantially positive impact on their kids' future, only 77% of parents feel their church involvement positively impacts their parenting.

In addition, over half (52%) of Christian parents report feeling like their faith community has trouble supporting their parenting. When asked to respond to the statement: *I feel that my faith community has*

→ Over half (52%) of Christian parents report feeling like their faith community has trouble supporting their parenting.

problems supporting my parenting, only 48% of Christian parents rated the statement untrue. These results may indicate that while Christian parents report higher levels of support than the average parenting population, many still feel the Church could be more supportive of their parenting.

In a follow up study, Christian parents were asked to provide more information about the ways they experience a lack of support at church.[23]

Half of all Christian parents say both pastors/clergy (51%) and members of the congregation/parish (49%) have trouble understanding the realities of their life. And some Christian parents say both pastors/clergy (42%) and members of the congregation/parish (49%) have trouble valuing them as a parent.

When asked to select areas where the Church could grow in empathy and understanding, a majority of Christian parents selected *every option provided*.

How Parents Feel Supported to Raise Kids with Faith and Character

In the values portion of this study, 95.5% of both Christian parents and the general population of parents said character development was *important* or *extremely important* to their parenting. But, how supported do parents feel in the task of raising kids to develop important values like honesty, trust, and love?

In general, parents feel less supported in their kids' character development than one might hope. One in four parents feel *extremely unable* to instill important character and values in their kids, and nearly half of all parents (44.2%) report some level of inability to successfully transfer important values.[24]

Ministry leaders may want to consider this question: Does faith impact character? If so, churches and parishes may be well-positioned to connect faith and character in a way that supports one of the overall greatest needs of parents.

Unlike parents' reported lack of support for character development, Christian parents say they feel more positive about their ability to pass faith on to their kids.

In a follow-up study, Christian parents were asked to complete the following statement: *"When it comes to passing faith on to my kids, I feel… "* The results? Only 1.4% of Christian parents feel *extremely unable* to nurture their kids' faith. This seems to suggest that a majority of Christian parents feel some level of competency in this area. Faith leaders may want to note, however, that 24.3% of highly committed Christian parents still say they feel *sometimes unable* to pass faith to their kids. In the next section we will explore some of the most helpful and least helpful sources for parents related to faith and character formation. And we will also report on specific suggestions from Christian parents about the kind of experiences and resources they want most.

Section 03 — How Parents Feel — What Most Parents Aren't Telling You

Parent Confidence for Raising Kids with Faith and Character

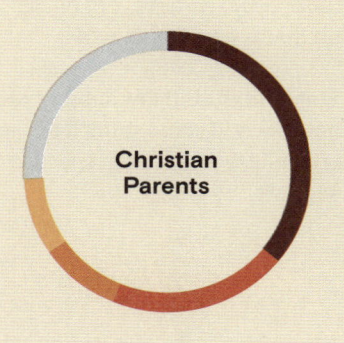

Christian Parents

Survey Statement
When it comes to instilling character in my kids, I feel…

35.8% Extremely Able
20.1% Often Able
9.4% Sometimes Able/Unable
8.7% Often Unable
26.1% Extremely Unable

Survey Statement
When it comes to passing faith on to my kids, I feel…

Extremely Able **31.9%**
Often Able **39%**
Sometimes Able/Unable **24.3%**
Often Unable **3.4%**
Extremely Unable **1.4%**

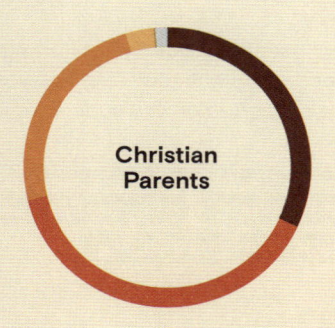

Christian Parents

n = 847 U.S. Christian parents with kids 0–25, March 2022

---

1 in 4 parents feel *extremely unable* to instill important character and values in their kids.

Nearly half of all parents (44.2%) reported some level of inability to successfully transfer important values.

n = 571 U.S. parents with kids 0–25, November/December 2020

What Parents Feel at Every Phase

As a child moves from birth through preschool, elementary, middle and high school, and into their young adult years, parents experience more than just their kid changing. Their level of support shifts as well.

Of the three least-supported areas for parents—college preparation, career readiness, and community involvement—only community involvement remains consistently least supported across every phase. Similarly, only one area of high support remains consistent across the phases: my friendship with my kids.

While high support areas tend to remain high, and low support areas tend to remain low across the phases, there are still some shifts from age group to age group. Below, we highlight the phase where each specific parent value reaches its lowest level of support.

For those who work with
→ Preschoolers

Summary
70.8% of parents of kids ages zero to three, and 73.2% of parents with four- and five-year-olds say they are *supported* or *well-supported* in every area.

Parental Support Lows with ages 0-3
- Career Readiness
- Physical Exercise
- Technological Responsibility

Notable
The largest value-to-support gap for this age group is career readiness, indicating parents may feel pressure to fuel their kids' future success right from the beginning.

■ Parents say *important* or *very important*
// Parents feel *supported* or *well-supported*

For those who work with
→ Elementary

Summary
71.7% of parents of kids ages six and seven years old, and 72.6% of parents of kids ages eight through eleven years old say they are *supported* or *well-supported* in every area.

Parental Support Lows with ages 6-7
- Access to Resources
- College Preparation
- Sexual Integrity
- Faith Development
- Extended Family Connections

Parental Support Lows with ages 8-11
- Access to Opportunities

Notable
One notable value-to-support gap for this age group is nutrition.

■ Parents say *important* or *very important*
// Parents feel *supported* or *well-supported*

Section 03   How Parents Feel   What Most Parents Aren't Telling You

For those who work with
→ **Middle Schoolers**

Summary
73.7% of parents of kids ages 12-15 years old say they are *supported* or *well-supported* in every area.

Parental Support Lows with ages 12-15
- My Friendship with My Kid
- Access to Opportunities

Value-to-Support Gaps with ages 12-15
- Healthy Mentors
- Career Readiness
- Mental Health
- Access to Opportunities

Notable
One notable value-to-support gap for this age group is mental health.

■ Parents say *important* or *very important*
/// Parents feel *supported* or *well-supported*

For those who work with
→ **High Schoolers**

Summary
74% of parents of kids ages 16-18 years old say they are *supported* or *well-supported* in every area.

Parental Support Lows with ages 16-18
- My Friendship with My Kid
- Physical Exercise

Value-to-Support Gaps with ages 16-18
- Healthy Mentors
- Career Readiness
- Mental Health
- Access to Opportunities
- Strong Friendships

Notable
One notable value-to-support gap for this age group is healthy mentors.

■ Parents say *important* or *very important*
/// Parents feel *supported* or *well-supported*

For those who work with
→ **Young Adults**

Summary
71.5% of parents of nineteen through twenty-three, and 78.6% of parents of twenty-four- and twenty-five-year-olds say they are *supported* or *well-supported* in every area.

Parental Support Lows with ages 19-25
- Healthy Mentors
- Educational Achievement
- Mental Health
- Character Development
- Strong Friendships
- Balanced Nutrition
- Faith Development*
- Community Involvement

Value-to-Support Gaps with ages 19-25
- Healthy Mentors
- Technological Responsibility
- Mental Health
- Access to Resources
- Strong Friendships
- Balanced Nutrition
- Career Readiness
- Access to Opportunities

*Faith Development is the only category pulled from Christian Parent findings rather than the general population study, and as such reflects when Christian parents feel least supported in their kids' faith development.

n = 1,464 U.S. parents with kids 0–25, June 2021

Key Findings: How Parents Feel

01
Christian parents feel more positive about how their church influences their kids' future than they feel about how their church influences their parenting.

02
62.1% of all parents say they know their kids more than other adults do. 26% of parents say other adults frequently don't understand their kids.

03
Parents with lower income report feeling *less supported* for thirteen of the seventeen areas of parenting.

04
Twice as many Christian parents as compared to all parents report feeling *supported* or *well-supported* in their kids' faith development. Those who attend faith services almost every week report higher levels of support than those who attend less frequently.

05
All parents report a high level of confidence in their ability to parent.

06
Over half (52%) of Christian parents report feeling like their faith community has trouble supporting their parenting.

07

Half of all Christian parents say both pastors/clergy (51%) and members of the congregation/parish (49%) have trouble understanding the realities of their life. Some Christian parents say both pastors/clergy (42%) and members of the congregation/parish (42.7%) have trouble valuing them as a parent.

08

1 in 4 parents feel extremely unable to instill important character and values in their kids, and nearly half of all parents (44.2%) report some level of inability to successfully transfer important values.

09

Most notably for youth leaders, Christian parents report feeling least supported to nurture their kids' faith after graduation.

10

Christian parents:
→ worry about their kids' faith most when their child is young (ages 4–11).
→ value their kids' faith most when their adolescent is growing (ages 12–18).
→ feel supported to nurture their kids' faith least when their kid is graduated (ages 19–25).

Parenting is a lot like folding a fitted sheet. No one really knows how to do it.

WHERE PARENTS GO FOR HELP

→ Every parent needs help. The task of raising a young person into adulthood is a big job. And, whether help shows up in the form of a neighbor, a teacher, a librarian, or another parent, a support network is an essential part of effective parenting.

Research shows that parents who have stable, high-quality support networks have increased responsiveness to their kids, higher parental satisfaction, and lower levels of anger, anxiety, and depression.[25] Moreover, social connection and concrete support for parents are linked to a lower incidence of child abuse and neglect.[26] Simply put, parents need people. It's important to have trustworthy relationships for sharing the joys, challenges, and surprises of parenthood.

These relationships also make space to exchange information and resources, as well as hope and encouragement. So, where do parents find the people and resources they need for support? Some parent support may come from early childhood institutions like child care centers and pre-K programs. Some essential parent support happens through intentional programming and activities at elementary, middle, and high schools. In fact, many studies indicate parents who build strong networks at the school level not only benefit from higher levels of relational and social capital but also develop a better understanding of the education system and more awareness of quality resources to aid in their decision-making.[27]

So, what does this mean for leaders who want to help parents successfully raise young people with a healthy sense of identity, belonging, and purpose? The first step is to begin by understanding what parents want, what they worry about, and how they feel, then to explore where they already find positive sources of help within the community. Only then is it possible to imagine new ways to create effective and integrated strategies for supporting parents in a more holistic way.

Section 04 — Where Parents Go For Help — What Most Parents Aren't Telling You

What Helps Parents Parent Their Kids

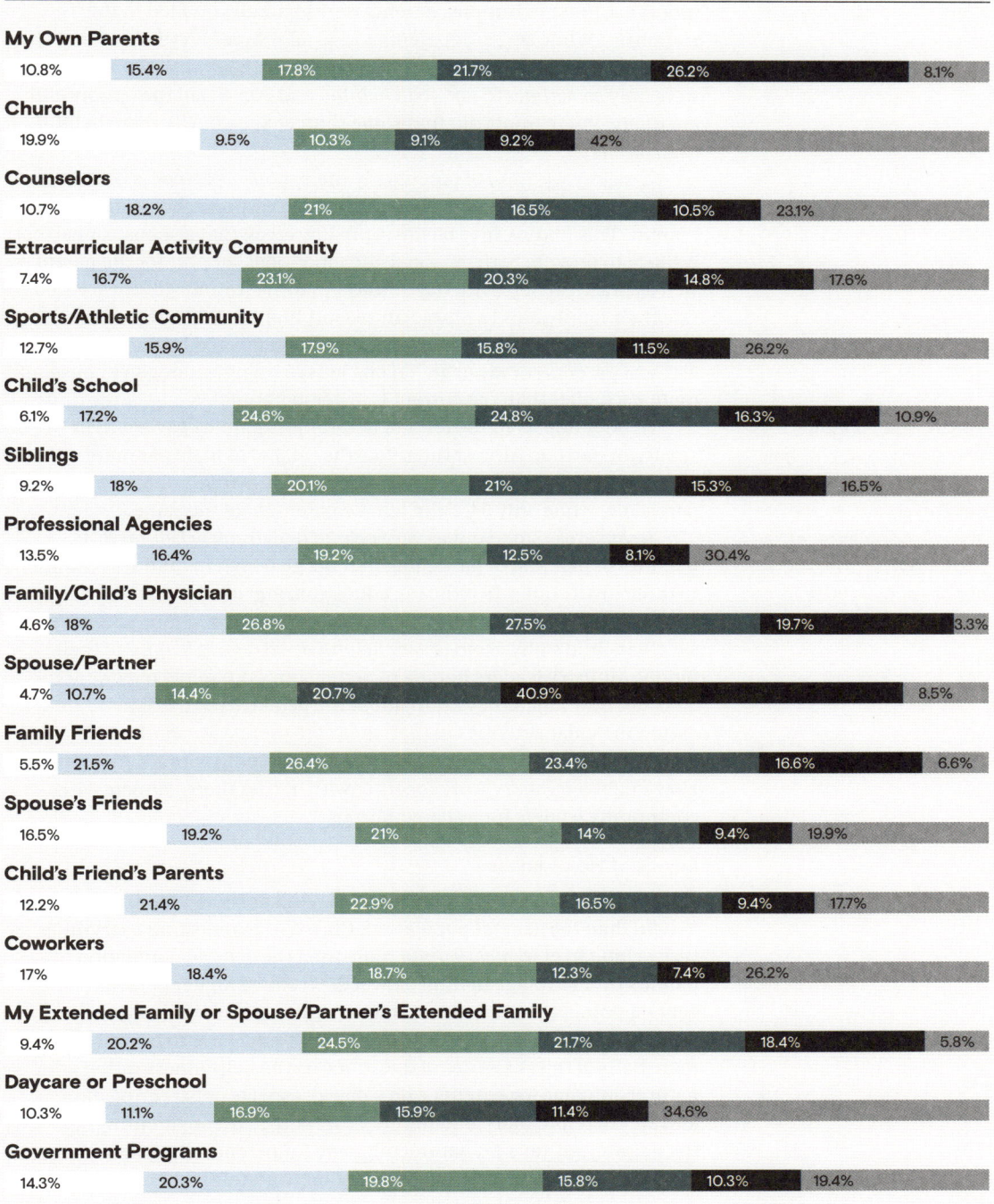

Legend:
- Not at all Helpful
- Sometimes Helpful
- Generally Helpful
- Very Helpful
- Extremely Helpful
- Not Applicable

My Own Parents
10.8% | 15.4% | 17.8% | 21.7% | 26.2% | 8.1%

Church
19.9% | 9.5% | 10.3% | 9.1% | 9.2% | 42%

Counselors
10.7% | 18.2% | 21% | 16.5% | 10.5% | 23.1%

Extracurricular Activity Community
7.4% | 16.7% | 23.1% | 20.3% | 14.8% | 17.6%

Sports/Athletic Community
12.7% | 15.9% | 17.9% | 15.8% | 11.5% | 26.2%

Child's School
6.1% | 17.2% | 24.6% | 24.8% | 16.3% | 10.9%

Siblings
9.2% | 18% | 20.1% | 21% | 15.3% | 16.5%

Professional Agencies
13.5% | 16.4% | 19.2% | 12.5% | 8.1% | 30.4%

Family/Child's Physician
4.6% | 18% | 26.8% | 27.5% | 19.7% | 3.3%

Spouse/Partner
4.7% | 10.7% | 14.4% | 20.7% | 40.9% | 8.5%

Family Friends
5.5% | 21.5% | 26.4% | 23.4% | 16.6% | 6.6%

Spouse's Friends
16.5% | 19.2% | 21% | 14% | 9.4% | 19.9%

Child's Friend's Parents
12.2% | 21.4% | 22.9% | 16.5% | 9.4% | 17.7%

Coworkers
17% | 18.4% | 18.7% | 12.3% | 7.4% | 26.2%

My Extended Family or Spouse/Partner's Extended Family
9.4% | 20.2% | 24.5% | 21.7% | 18.4% | 5.8%

Daycare or Preschool
10.3% | 11.1% | 16.9% | 15.9% | 11.4% | 34.6%

Government Programs
14.3% | 20.3% | 19.8% | 15.8% | 10.3% | 19.4%

n = 1,464 U.S. parents with kids 0–25, June 2021

Humans Need Help Raising Humans

Parents are better parents when they have the right kind of help. When asked to rate the level of helpfulness for a series of relationships, programs, and institutions, parents were generally divided in their responses. While 30.2% of parents found all sources *very helpful* or *extremely helpful*, 20% said they were *generally helpful*, 28.7% said they were only *sometimes* to *not at all helpful*, and 20.1% said the options did *not apply*. But, parents did find some sources specifically more helpful than others.

A majority (61.1%) of parents say their spouse/partner is *very helpful* or *extremely helpful*, making this the leading response by a significant margin. This finding may be unsurprising, given that a spouse or partner is likely to provide both personal and emotional support for the parent as well as practical help with day-to-day parenting responsibilities. Parents rate their family/child's physician second-highest (47.2%) by comparison. The helpfulness of a spouse or partner is underscored by the fact that 25.7% of parents surveyed are raising kids in a single-caregiver household (only 2% higher than the current U.S. demographic).[28]

Gender impacted the level of helpfulness parents gave to their spouse or partner. Almost three-fourths (74.5%) of male parents said their spouse/partner was a *very helpful* or *extremely helpful* source for their parenting, while only 54.2% of female parents said the same.

Seven areas stood out as *very helpful* or *extremely helpful* to a majority of parents. In particular, parents give high helpfulness ratings to three institutions: healthcare, education, and extracurricular communities like art, drama, or music. Nearly three in four parents say their child's physician is *very helpful* or *extremely helpful* to their family. Ministry leaders hoping to better support parents may want to consider how much they know about the pediatricians, teachers, and extra-curricular activities in their area. Are there ways ministries might partner with organizations that are already helping parents and families? How might a ministry work together with, rather than compete with, community leaders for a shared purpose?

→ Christian parents rate every source of help *very helpful* or *extremely helpful* more than the general population of parents by an average margin of over 20%.

Levels of Helpfulness

By way of contrast, Christian parents view all areas of support as *more helpful* than the general population. Christian parents find everything *very helpful* to *extremely helpful* more than the general population of parents by an average margin of over 20%. And a higher percent of general population parents compared to Christian parents rated every area *unhelpful*. The propensity Christian parents have to rate all areas more helpful raises a series of questions. Is the helpfulness rating a natural outcome for parents who value all aspects of parenting more, and are therefore more intentional in seeking help for parenting? Is the helpfulness rating a natural outcome for parents who worry about their parenting more often, so they are more grateful for help when they

Levels of Helpfulness

How parents rate all 17 sources of parenting help on average.

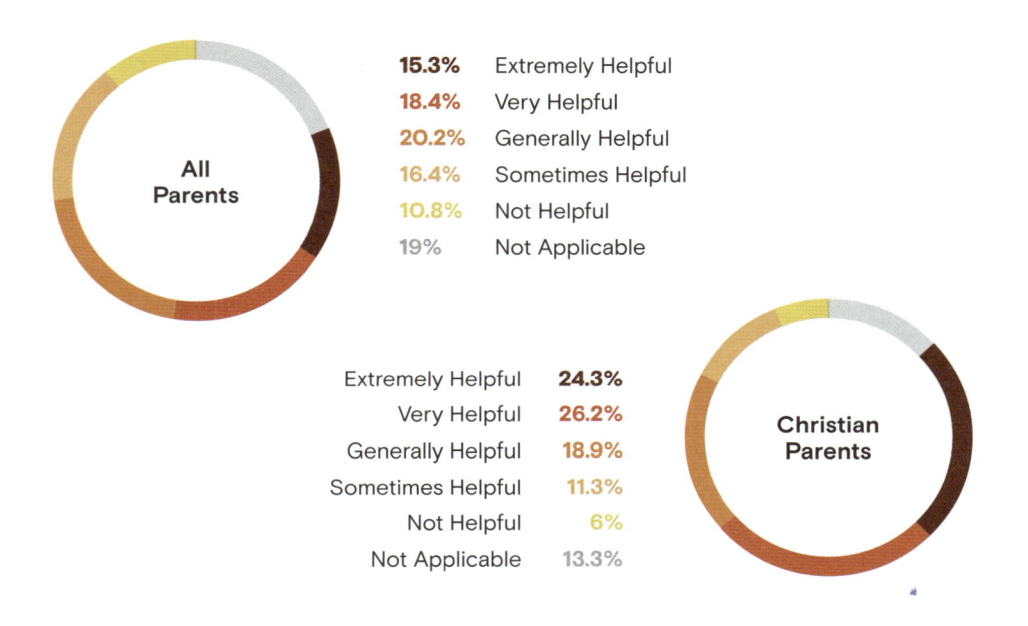

All Parents

15.3%	Extremely Helpful
18.4%	Very Helpful
20.2%	Generally Helpful
16.4%	Sometimes Helpful
10.8%	Not Helpful
19%	Not Applicable

Christian Parents

Extremely Helpful	**24.3%**
Very Helpful	**26.2%**
Generally Helpful	**18.9%**
Sometimes Helpful	**11.3%**
Not Helpful	**6%**
Not Applicable	**13.3%**

n = 1,464 U.S. parents with kids 0–25, June 2021
n = 1,269 U.S. Christian parents with kids 0–25, February 2022

---

find it? Is there something else about faith generally that engenders appreciation for supporting relationships, resources, and organizations? Perhaps it's all or none of these, but ministry leaders who work with parents may have a unique opportunity to win with Christian parents when they connect them to help for their parenting.

Where Parents Go for Help Most

So, the real question is: Where do parents turn when they need help in parenting? This study sought to discover that answer by asking two related questions. First, "Where does the majority of your support as a caregiver come from?" Parents were given the opportunity to select up to three from a list of twelve options in order to limit the areas they turn to most often. Second, "Have you ever consulted any of the following for support as a caregiver?" Parents were presented with the same list of twelve options and asked to select all that apply. The response to both questions produced similar results and demonstrated that a majority of parents are actively seeking help in many places.

The place parents go for help most often is the same place they rated most helpful: a spouse/partner. Over half (81.7%) of parents say they have consulted a spouse or partner for parenting help, and only 14% of parents say they have consulted neither a current nor ex-partner for parenting help. These findings emphasize the significance of a co-parenting role, where applicable, in helping parents have the help they need as they raise the kids in their home.

Parents give mixed reviews about the helpfulness of online communities like YouTube and Facebook. Less than 50% of parents say they have consulted a social network platform for help, and more than 50% of parents say they have never visited these platforms seeking help for parenting. And parents still respond in favor of books (57.6%) over podcasts (21.9%) when it comes to help for their parenting.

More female parents than male parents say they have consulted friends, neighbors, and extended family for parenting help. This may be an indicator that male parents are less inclined to turn to relational networks outside the home for help with their parenting.

→ Parents give mixed reviews about the helpfulness of online communities like YouTube and Facebook.

All Parents' Top Five Sources
#1 Spouse/Partner
#2 Extended Family
#3 Friends & Neighbors
#4 Internet Searches
#5 Books

All Parents' "Have Consulted"
#1 Spouse/Partner
#2 Extended Family
#3 Friends & Neighbors
#4 Internet Searches
#5 Books

Christian Parents' Top Five Sources
#1 Spouse/Partner
#2 Extended Family
#3 Church
#4 Friends & Neighbors
#5 Internet Searches

Christian Parents' "Have Consulted"
#1 Spouse/Partner
#2 Extended Family
#3 Church
#4 Friends & Neighbors
#5 Books

All parents look for parenting help from someone they know before turning to other resources. Parents say they look first to a spouse/partner and then to extended family. Christian parents do not differ from the general population in where they go for help with one encouraging distinction—the Church. Nearly three out of every four Christian parents say they have consulted their church or parish for parenting help. And 41.6% of Christian parents selected Church as a top-three source for parenting help.

Christian parents have consulted every source more often than the general population. Of the twelve options provided in this study, no source of help received less than a 30% rating from Christian parents. If 30% of Christian parents have consulted *every* source, it may indicate a need to consider more than one approach when helping parents.

→ Christian parents do not differ from the general population in where they go for help with one encouraging distinction—the Church.

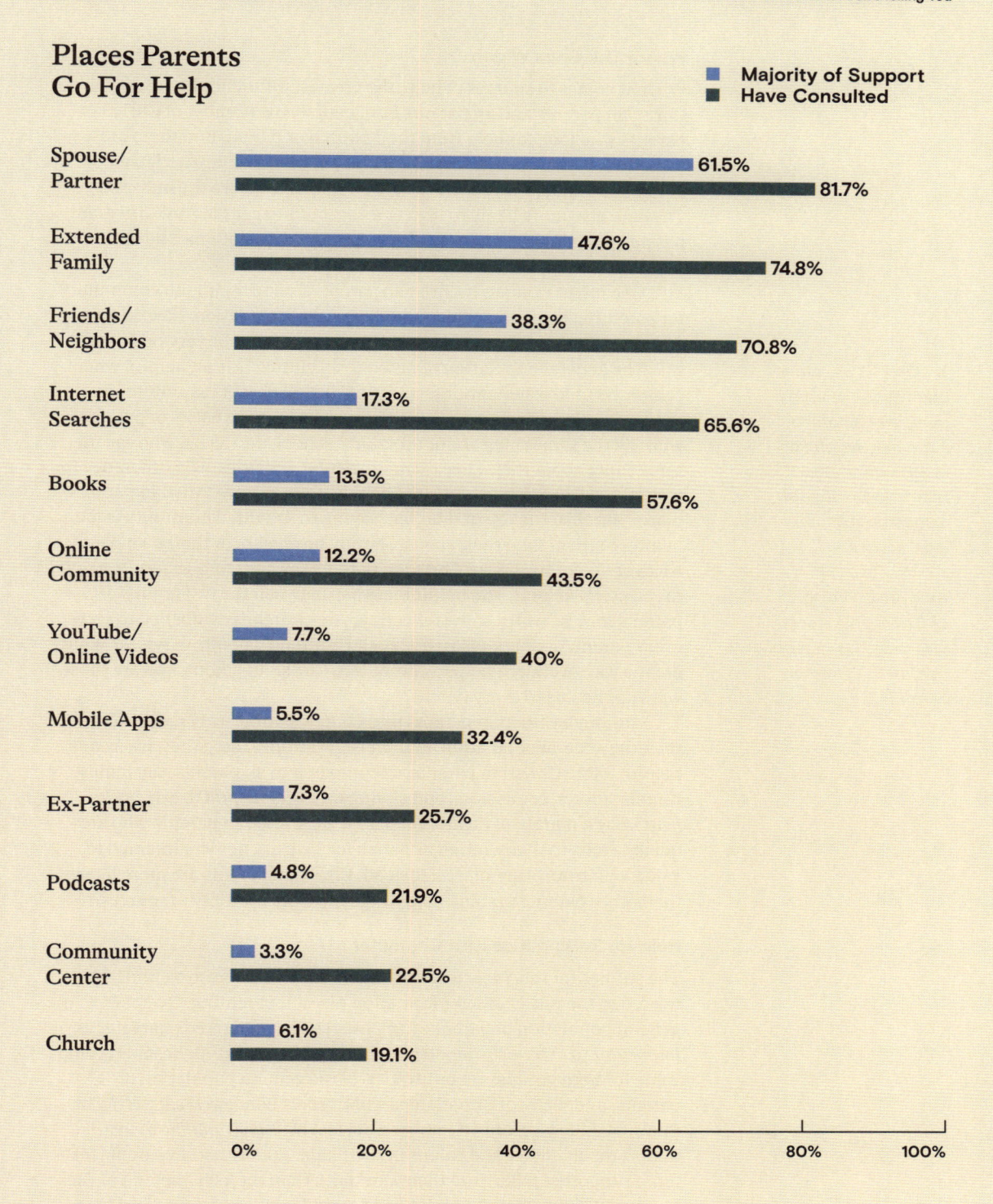

Section 04 · Where Parents Go For Help · What Most Parents Aren't Telling You

Places Parents Go For Help

■ Majority of Support
■ Have Consulted

Source	Majority of Support	Have Consulted
Spouse/Partner	61.5%	81.7%
Extended Family	47.6%	74.8%
Friends/Neighbors	38.3%	70.8%
Internet Searches	17.3%	65.6%
Books	13.5%	57.6%
Online Community	12.2%	43.5%
YouTube/Online Videos	7.7%	40%
Mobile Apps	5.5%	32.4%
Ex-Partner	7.3%	25.7%
Podcasts	4.8%	21.9%
Community Center	3.3%	22.5%
Church	6.1%	19.1%

n = 1,464 U.S. parents with kids 0–25, June 2021

Where The Gaps Widen

When it comes to sources of help, the greatest difference between Christian parents and all parents is, of course, the number of Christian parents who look for help from their church or parish. But, there are a few other distinctions as well. Christian parents, as compared to all parents, are more likely to have consulted books before the internet. They are also more likely to turn to a community center. And Christian parents indicate higher levels of engagement with both mobile apps and podcasts.

One might wonder: If Christian parents turn to their faith community for parenting help more often than the general population, how do they feel about the help they receive? The answer seems to be very positive.

The general population of parents say church is least helpful when compared to 16 other options. Only 21.5% of all parents say church is *generally helpful* or *extremely helpful*, as compared to 63.6% of parents who say the same thing about their kids' school, and 55.8% who say the same thing about their kids' extra-curricular activities. The difference for committed Christian parents is shocking. Committed Christian parents place church at the top of their list, saying their faith community is more helpful to them than their spouse, family physician, or their own parents. An overwhelming 88% of Christian parents say church is *generally helpful* to *extremely helpful*. The helpfulness gap between the two groups of parents may be worth some reflection. Are churches compelled to serve every parent, or only those who regularly attend worship services? What are the ways a church helps a committed Christian parent, and are those ways applicable to every parent?

Although Christian parents find church significantly more helpful than the general population, church isn't the only thing they see as more helpful. More Christian parents, as compared to all parents, say family friends, sports, counselors, and siblings are *very helpful* to *extremely helpful* by a margin of greater than 20%. So, Christian parents who are quick to look to their church or parish for help are not less inclined to value help from other places. Instead, Christian parents are more likely than other parents to value parenting help from a variety of sources.

Help for Raising Kids with Character

The studies for this project revealed a number of interesting findings related to the role character formation plays in parenting. Over 95% of the general population of parents and Christian parents rated character as *important* to *extremely important*, making it the third-highest parenting value for both groups. Yet only 69.9% of the general population of parents, and 49.1% of Christian parents, report being *well-supported* in this area. Likewise, one in four parents feel *extremely unable* to instill important character and values in their kids. And Christian parents feel more supported to nurture their kids' faith than their character. For these reasons, it's important to specifically consider where parents find help raising kids with character.

→ Only 21.5% of all parents say church is *generally helpful* or *extremely helpful* as compared to 63.6% of parents who say the same about their kids' school.

An overwhelming 88% of Christian parents say church is *generally helpful* to *extremely helpful*.

Parents Differ in Where They Go for Help

The percent of parents who say they have consulted these sources for parenting help.

All Parents

22.5%	Community Center	
21.9%	Podcasts	
32.4%	Mobile Apps	

Christian Parents

	Community Center	41.5%
	Podcasts	32.9%
	Mobile Apps	40.4%

n = 1,464 U.S. parents with kids 0–25, June 2021
n = 1,269 U.S. Christian parents with kids 0–25, February 2022

Parents Differ in How They Appreciate Help

The percent of parents who found these sources *very helpful* or *extremely helpful*.

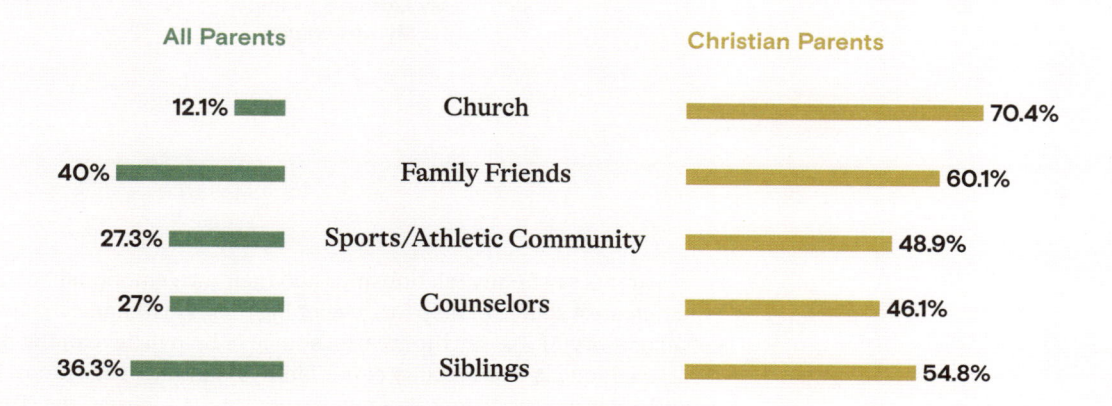

All Parents

12.1%	Church	
40%	Family Friends	
27.3%	Sports/Athletic Community	
27%	Counselors	
36.3%	Siblings	

Christian Parents

	Church	70.4%
	Family Friends	60.1%
	Sports/Athletic Community	48.9%
	Counselors	46.1%
	Siblings	54.8%

n = 1,464 U.S. parents with kids 0–25, June 2021
n = 1,269 U.S. Christian parents with kids 0–25, February 2022

Helpful Resources for Character Development

The percent of parents who say each source is *most helpful* for raising kids with character.

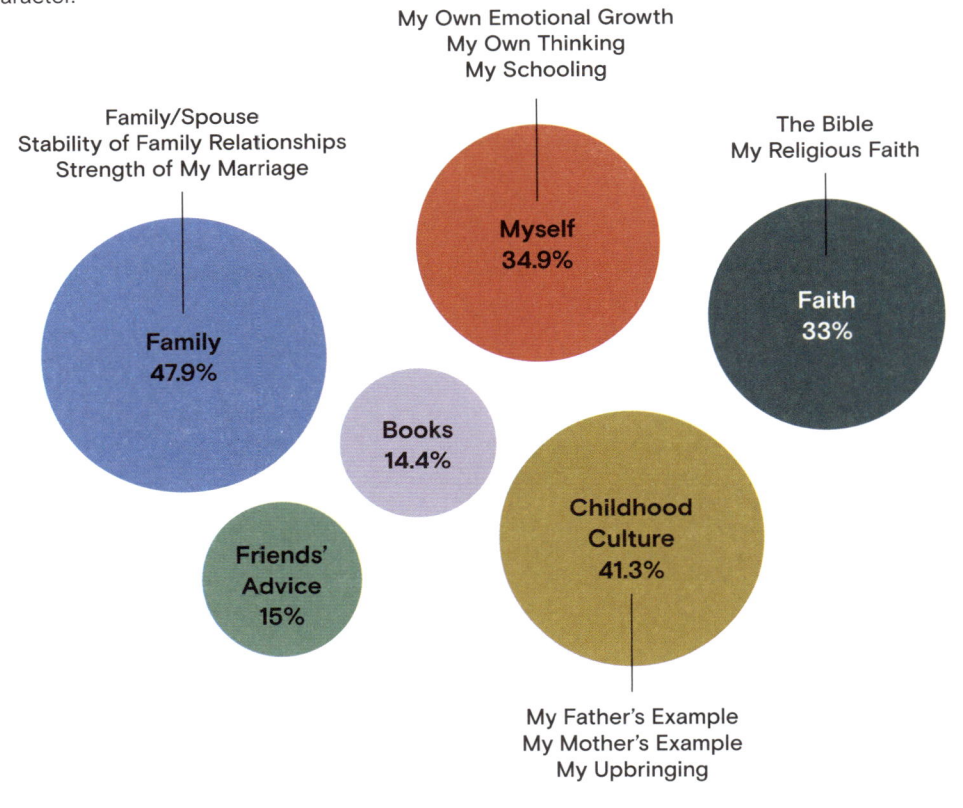

Family/Spouse
Stability of Family Relationships
Strength of My Marriage

Family 47.9%

My Own Emotional Growth
My Own Thinking
My Schooling

Myself 34.9%

The Bible
My Religious Faith

Faith 33%

Books 14.4%

Friends' Advice 15%

Childhood Culture 41.3%

My Father's Example
My Mother's Example
My Upbringing

n = 571 U.S. parents with kids 0–25, November/December 2020

Parents say family relationships and their own emotional health are their greatest source of help for developing their kids' character. Over half of all parents (51.5%) say the greatest source of help in developing their kids' character is "the stability of our family relationships." Almost half (48.5%) also say the "support of my partner" and 43.7% say "the strength of my marriage" is also helpful.

Second to family relationships, roughly two in five parents say they are their own best source of help, citing "my own emotional growth," "my father's example," "my mother's example," and "my upbringing" as key areas of support for raising kids with character. This second tier of responses may indicate parents' overall awareness of the importance of modeling character as a method for influencing their kids' character formation.

All parents say their own education, the Bible, books on parenting, and the advice of a friend are more *unhelpful* than *helpful* for nurturing their kids' character.

Parents report a number of obstacles to nurturing their kids' character—namely, the same things that have the potential to be their greatest source of help. Parents name lack of support from family, followed by their own emotional health as the top potential obstacles when it comes to nurturing their kids' character. Almost half of all parents (45.4%) say the greatest barrier to raising their kids with character is the lack of support from their extended family. And 34.4% say their greatest barrier is lack of support from a spouse/partner.

Second, behind the lack of support from extended family, parents say they are their own greatest barrier. More than 38% of parents say "my own emotional issues" are the biggest problem. Comparatively, parents do not see their low energy or their child's resistance as an obstacle. These responses indicate that parents and kids are likely willing to work on character development, but may not have the personal and relational help necessary for the work.

A relatively strong 33.3% of parents say their greatest obstacle to nurturing their kids' character is they simply "don't know how," and 31% say their greatest obstacle is they "never had this modeled for them." These responses further support the idea that a number of parents may be open to training in this area. These findings also show that parents feel most capable to nurture their kids' character when they have stable nuclear and extended family relationships. It may be that efforts to nurture family relationships will tangentially impact a parent's ability to nurture their kids' character.

Help for Raising Kids with Faith

Similar to findings about the role of character formation for U.S. parents, the studies for this project also revealed a number of interesting things about the way parents view faith and church. To recap, 94.3% of Christian parents say their kids' faith is *important* or *extremely important*. Most Christian parents (70%) say they worry *somewhat*, *often*, or *all of the time* about their kids' faith. More than half (63%) of Christian parents say consistent connection to a faith community is an essential part of their family, and 61.7% of Christian parents say they attend religious services almost every week. A little more than half (54%) of Christian parents say they are *well-supported* in nurturing their kids faith development. But 29% of highly committed Christian parents still say they feel *extremely*, *often*, or *sometimes unable* to pass faith to their kids. For these reasons, it's important to specifically explore the sources of help and potential obstacles for parents who wish to instill faith in their kids.

→ Parents say family relationships and their own emotional health are their greatest source of help for developing their kids' character.

→ Parents name lack of support from family, followed by their own emotional health as the top potential obstacles when it comes to nurturing their kids' character.

> Christian parents say "who they are" and "how they are connected" matters more than "what they have" when it comes to influencing their kids' faith.

> Christian parents indicate feeling like they are their own biggest barrier to their kids' spiritual formation.

> Interest in Mentors, Resources, Prompts and Practical Training was higher in parents who attend church more often.

During a follow-up study, Christian parents were asked to reflect on the most and least helpful sources for raising kids with faith. And here's what they said: Christian parents say "who they are" and "how they are connected" matters more than "what they have" when it comes to influencing their kids' faith.

Over half of Christian parents say the Bible and their own spiritual growth are the most important in helping them nurture their kids' faith. Only 15.8% of Christian parents say their personal spiritual growth is least helpful, indicating a strong level of personal ownership in the process of spiritual formation.

Christian parents also place a high value on personal relationships. Half (50.6%) of Christian parents say their current church or parish and 42.7% say the support of their spouse/partner is most helpful. In some responses, Christian parents give mixed results. Presumably, areas like their own upbringing, memories from church, and influence of grandparents may be helpful for some, and less helpful for others.

Apart from the Bible, Christian parents rate all resources as less important to nurturing their kids' faith than their own spiritual growth and relational support.

When asked about barriers to nurturing their kids' faith, Christian parents again reflect a high level of personal ownership. Christian parents indicate feeling like they are their own biggest barrier to their kids' spiritual formation. Compared to the 52.5% of Christian parents who say their own spiritual growth matters most in helping them nurture their kids' faith, 34.8% of Christian parents say "my low energy," 31.9% say "my lack of time to participate in church," and 26.6% say "my own spiritual issues" are the greatest obstacles in helping nurture their kids' faith. While the high level of personal ownership may be an indicator that Christian parents desire to do more, it may also reflect a high level of shame for some who perceive they are the barrier to giving their kids the faith they desire for them.

When evaluating their time, Christian parents say their lack of time for church is a greater obstacle than their lack of time for parenting when it comes to nurturing their kids' faith. After all, Christian parents did describe themselves as nurturing, present, responsive, and engaged. If parents are present and engaged at home, and time to parent is not an obstacle, then ministry leaders may want to consider more ways to help parents nurture faith at home. How might Christian parents grow in their own faith and connection to a faith community beyond weekly church attendance? Are there ways to resource parents for better day-to-day faith conversations so discipleship happens in a flexible and consistent rhythm throughout the week?

A sizable 23.9% of Christian parents say their greatest obstacle to nurturing their kids' faith is they simply "don't know how," indicating that a number of parents may be open to training in this area.

Section 04   Where Parents Go For Help   What Most Parents Aren't Telling You

Helpful Resources for Faith Development

The percent of parents who say each resource is helpful for raising kids with faith.

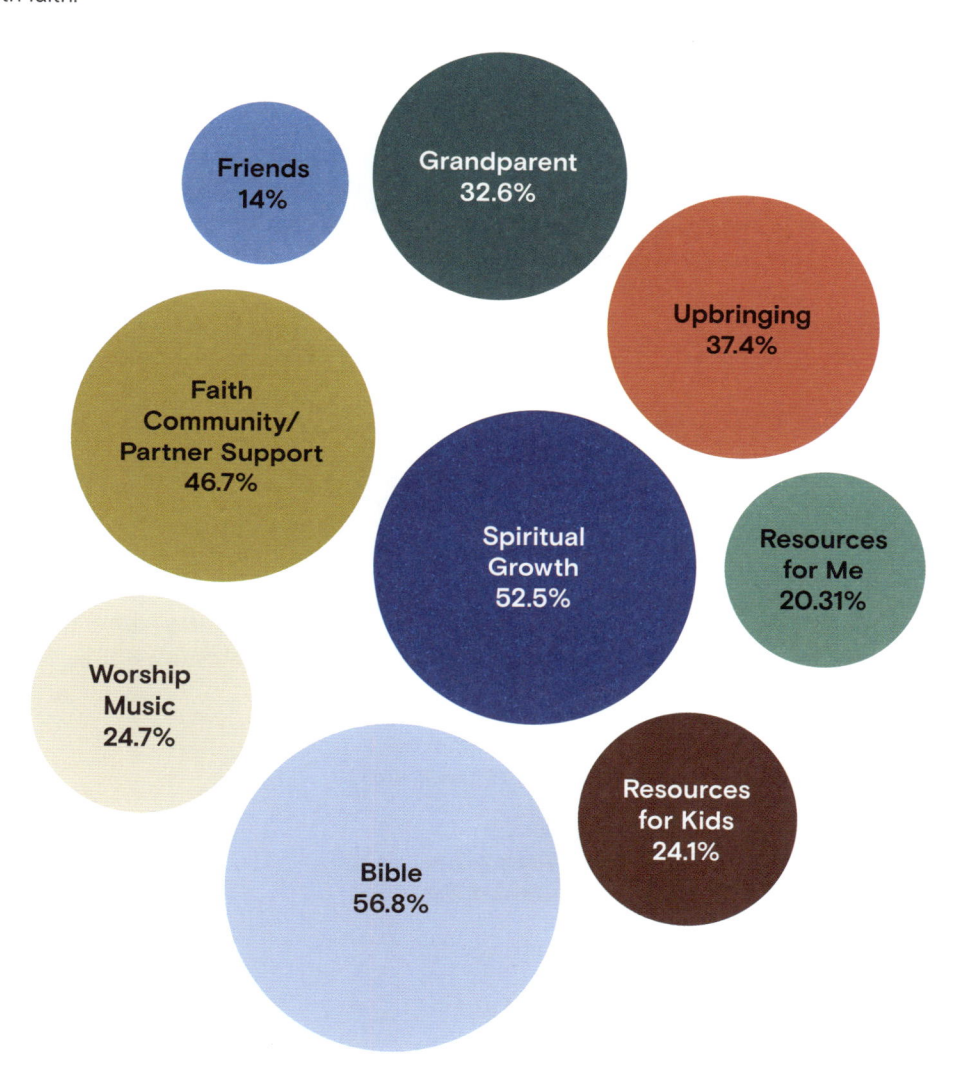

- Friends 14%
- Grandparent 32.6%
- Upbringing 37.4%
- Faith Community/Partner Support 46.7%
- Spiritual Growth 52.5%
- Resources for Me 20.31%
- Worship Music 24.7%
- Bible 56.8%
- Resources for Kids 24.1%

n = 571 U.S. parents with kids 0–25, November/December 2020

Ideas to Help Every Parent

Both parents in general and Christian parents were asked which resources they would like to have *more of* as a parent. In their responses, no resource received less than 20% indicating that a strong number of parents are looking for more help with their parenting.

A large majority (62.7%) of parents say they want more family experiences to attend together. This response remains consistently high for parents of middle school, high school, and young adult kids. This parent desire may be unsurprising, given the potential of shared experiences to create strong emotional and relational connections. Ministry leaders who primarily create age-specific programming may want to consider new opportunities to design shared experiences for family connection.

Following shared experiences, 40.6% of parents say they would like more resources to help them understand their kids at every phase, and 38.6% of parents want more prompts to help them have better conversations with their kids at home.

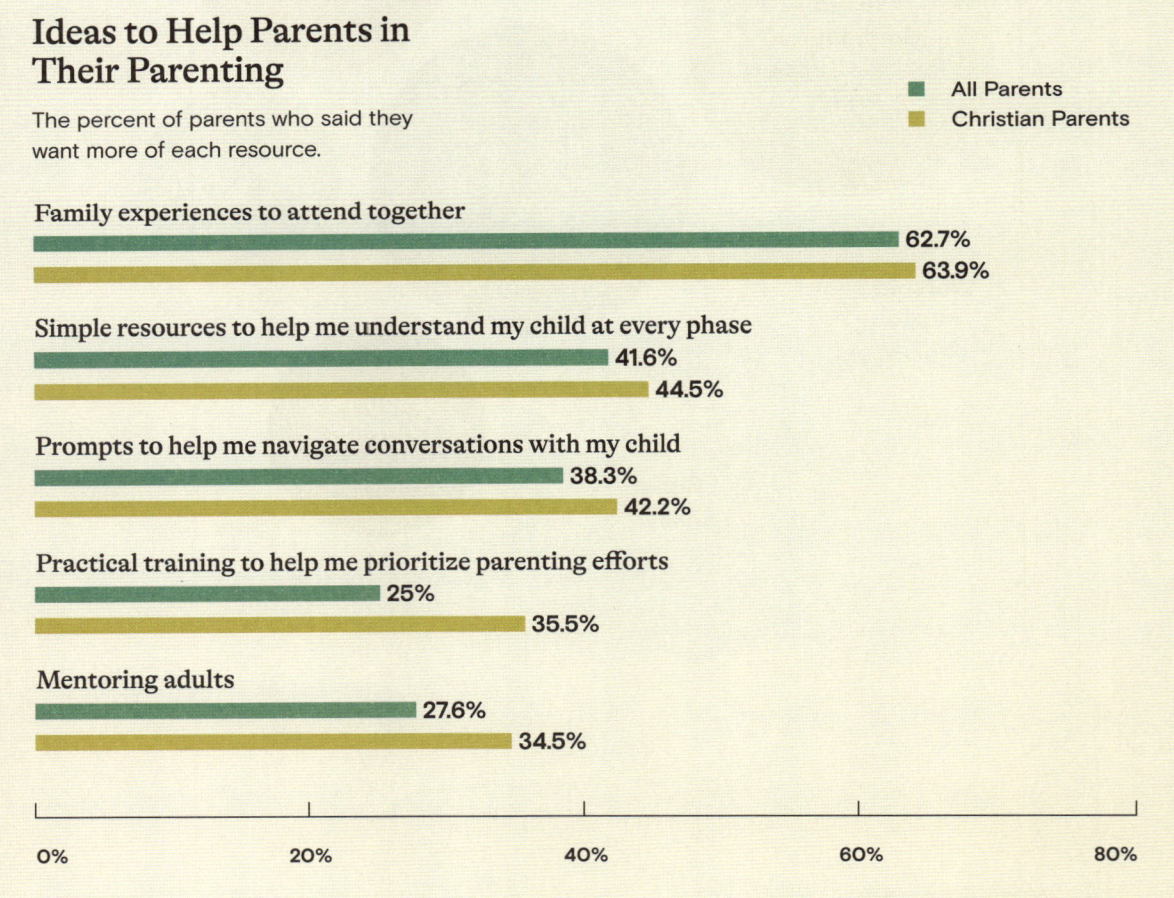

Ideas to Help Parents in Their Parenting

The percent of parents who said they want more of each resource.

- All Parents
- Christian Parents

Family experiences to attend together
- All Parents: 62.7%
- Christian Parents: 63.9%

Simple resources to help me understand my child at every phase
- All Parents: 41.6%
- Christian Parents: 44.5%

Prompts to help me navigate conversations with my child
- All Parents: 38.3%
- Christian Parents: 42.2%

Practical training to help me prioritize parenting efforts
- All Parents: 25%
- Christian Parents: 35.5%

Mentoring adults
- All Parents: 27.6%
- Christian Parents: 34.5%

n = 1,464 U.S. parents with kids 0–25, June 2021
n = 1,269 U.S. Christian parents with kids 0–25, February 2022

Ideas to Help Parents Raise Kids with Faith

The percent of Christian parents who said they want more of each resource.

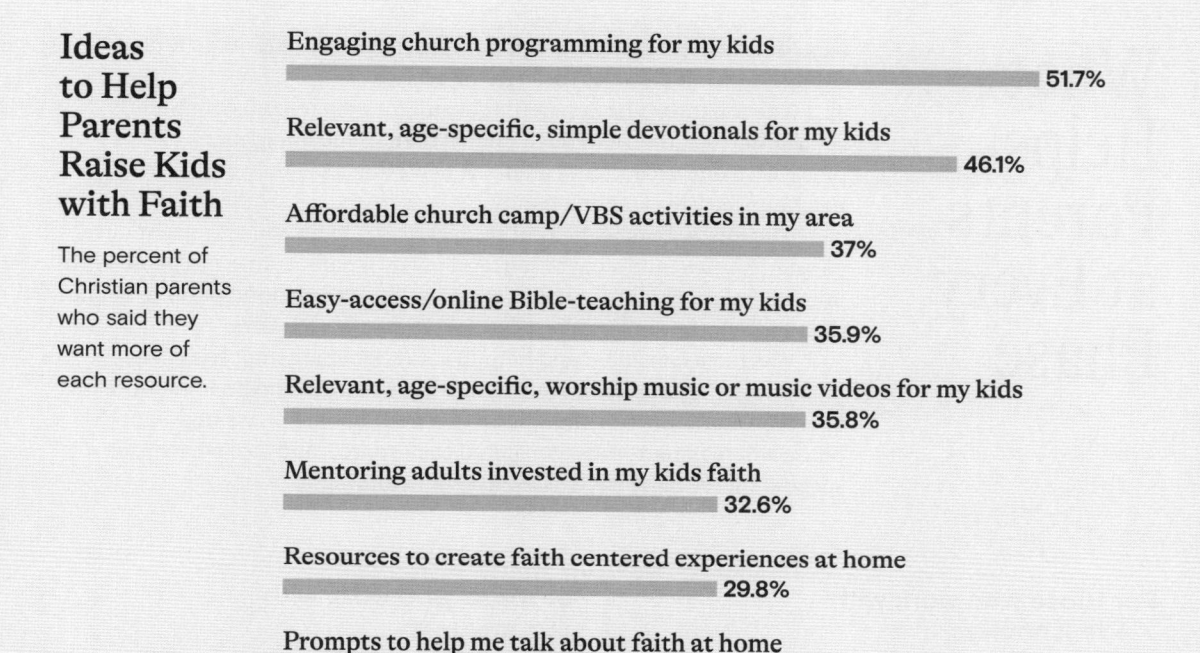

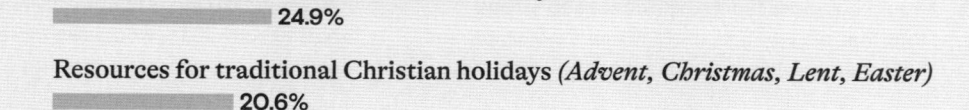

- Engaging church programming for my kids — **51.7%**
- Relevant, age-specific, simple devotionals for my kids — **46.1%**
- Affordable church camp/VBS activities in my area — **37%**
- Easy-access/online Bible-teaching for my kids — **35.9%**
- Relevant, age-specific, worship music or music videos for my kids — **35.8%**
- Mentoring adults invested in my kids faith — **32.6%**
- Resources to create faith centered experiences at home — **29.8%**
- Prompts to help me talk about faith at home — **26.8%**
- Practical training on how I can influence my kids' faith at home — **24.9%**
- Resources for traditional Christian holidays *(Advent, Christmas, Lent, Easter)* — **20.6%**

n = 847 U.S. Christian parents with kids 0–25, March 2022

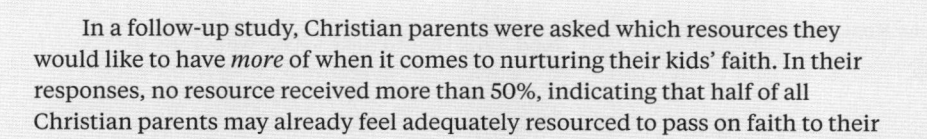

In a follow-up study, Christian parents were asked which resources they would like to have *more* of when it comes to nurturing their kids' faith. In their responses, no resource received more than 50%, indicating that half of all Christian parents may already feel adequately resourced to pass on faith to their kids. And no resource received less than 20%, indicating that a strong number of Christian parents are still looking for more help in this area.

Interestingly, although Christian parents say their own spiritual growth is most helpful for passing faith to their kids, Christian parents consistently favor resources for their kids over resources for themselves. Perhaps this reflects parents' emphasis on helping their kids more than helping themselves. Or, perhaps Christian parents feel resourced for their own spiritual development, but lacking in age-appropriate or relevant discipleship resources for their kids.

Either way, over half of Christian parents say the thing they want most is engaging church programs for their kids. Secondly, they want relevant, age-specific, simple devotionals for their kids.

What Helps Parents at Every Phase

Just like every other aspect of parenting, the places parents go for help changes as a child moves through the phases.

The top three places parents consult for help remain consistently spouse/partner, then extended family, then friends/neighbors, in every phase with one exception. Parents of new babies say they often turn to neighbors before extended family.

The top three most helpful sources also remain consistently spouse/partner, family/child's physician, and my own parents in every phase with one exception. Parents say their child's school is as helpful or more helpful than their family/child's physician for the first seven years.

The most consulted and helpful sources remain high across the phases, and the least consulted and helpful sources remain low, but there are still some shifts from age group to age group. Below, we highlight the phase where parents most consulted each source, and also where each specific source reached its peak level of helpfulness.

For those who work with
→ **Preschoolers**

Summary
67.1% of parents of kids ages zero to five say they would like more family experiences to attend together, and 40.5% would like more prompts to help them navigate conversations with their kid.

Consulted Source Peaks with ages 0-5
- Spouse/Partner
- Friends/Neighbors
- Internet Searches
- Online Community
- YouTube/Online Videos
- Mobile Apps

Resources Helpfulness Peaks with ages 0-5
- Preschool/Daycare

Notable
More parents turn to a spouse/partner in this phase than in any other.

- ■ Parents have consulted a spouse/partner
- ∕∕ Parents say spouse/partner is very helpful or extremely helpful

For those who work with
→ **Elementary**

Summary
66.1% of parents of kids ages six to eleven say they would like more family experiences to attend together, and 45.1% would like more simple resources to understand their kid at every phase.

Consulted Source Peaks with ages 6-11
- Extended Family
- Friends and Neighbors
- Books
- YouTube/Online Videos
- Ex-Partner
- Podcasts

Resources Helpfulness Peaks with ages 6-11
- Spouse/Partner
- Family/Child's physician
- Child's School
- Extended Family
- Coworkers

Notable
More parents say they have consulted sources for parenting help in this phase than any other.

- Extended Family
- Friends/Neighbors
- Books
- Ex-Partner
- Podcasts
- YouTube or Online Video

Section 04 — Where Parents Go For Help — What Most Parents Aren't Telling You

For those who work with
→ **Middle Schoolers**

Summary
60.1% of parents of kids ages twelve to fifteen say they would like more family experiences to attend together, and 40.9% would like more simple resources to understand their kid at every phase.

Consulted Source Peaks with ages 12-15
- Church/Parish

Resources Helpfulness Peaks with ages 12-15
- Extra-Curricular Activities
- Church/Parish
- Government Programs

Notable
More parents in the general population turn to a church for parenting help in this phase than in any other.

01/04

For those who work with
→ **High Schoolers**

Summary
57.9% of parents of kids ages sixteen to eighteen say they would like more family experiences to attend together, and 37% would like more prompts to help them navigate conversations with their kid.

Consulted Source Peaks with ages 16-18
- Church/Parish

Resources Helpfulness Peaks with ages 16-18
- My Own Parents
- Family Friends
- Siblings
- Counselors
- Child's Friend's Parents
- Government Programs

Notable*
Parents turn to more personal sources for help as their kid moves into adolescent phases.

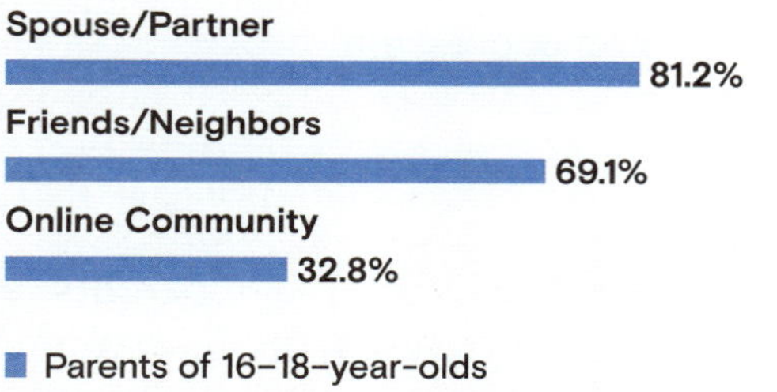

Spouse/Partner — 81.2%
Friends/Neighbors — 69.1%
Online Community — 32.8%

■ Parents of 16–18-year-olds

For those who work with
→ **Young Adults**

Summary
63.1% of parents of kids ages nineteen to twenty-five say they would like more family experiences to attend together, and 41.3% would like more simple resources to understand their young adult.

Consulted Source Peaks with ages 19-25
- Community Center

Resources Helpfulness Peaks with ages 19-25
- Sports/Athletic Community
- Spouse's Friends
- Coworkers

Notable*
Parents find sports and athletic communities increasingly helpful over time.

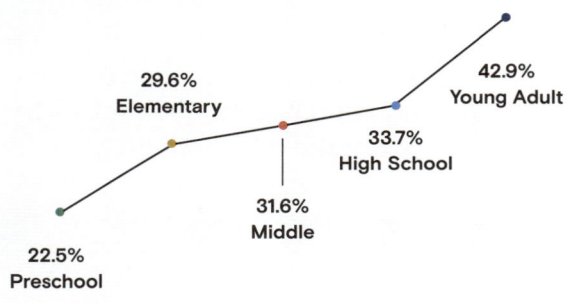

- 22.5% Preschool
- 29.6% Elementary
- 31.6% Middle
- 33.7% High School
- 42.9% Young Adult

n = 1,464 U.S. parents with kids 0–25, June 2021 *Percent of parents who have consulted these sources for parenting help.

Key Findings: Where Parents Go For Help

01

Research shows that parents who have stable, high-quality support networks have increased responsiveness to their kids, higher parental satisfaction, and lower levels of anger, anxiety, and depression.

02

A majority (61.1%) of parents say their spouse/partner is extremely helpful, making this the leading response by a significant margin. Parents rate their family or child's physician second highest (47.2%) by comparison.

03

The general population of parents say church is least helpful when compared to sixteen other options.

04

The place parents go for help most often is the same place they rate most helpful: a spouse or partner. 81.7% of parents say they have consulted a spouse or partner for parenting help, and only 14% of parents say they have consulted neither a current nor ex-partner for parenting help.

05

Christian parents do not differ from the general population in where they go for help with one encouraging distinction—the Church.

06

Parents say family relationships and their own emotional health are their greatest source of help for developing their kids' character.

07

Parents give high helpfulness ratings to three institutions: healthcare, education, and extracurricular communities like art, drama, or music.

08

Just like every other aspect of parenting, the places parents go for help change as a child moves from birth through preschool, elementary, middle, and finally high school.

09

Although Christian parents say their own spiritual growth is most helpful for passing faith to their kids, Christian parents consistently favor resources for their kids over resources for themselves.

10

When Christian parents and all parents were asked which resources they would like to have *more of* as a parent, no resource received less than 20%, indicating a strong number of parents are looking for more help with their parenting.

11

Parents are more likely to conduct internet searches and access help through mobile apps during the first three years than at any other phase.

Section 04   Open Ended   What Most Parents Aren't Telling You

If you could do anything at all to make the world better for your kids what would you do?

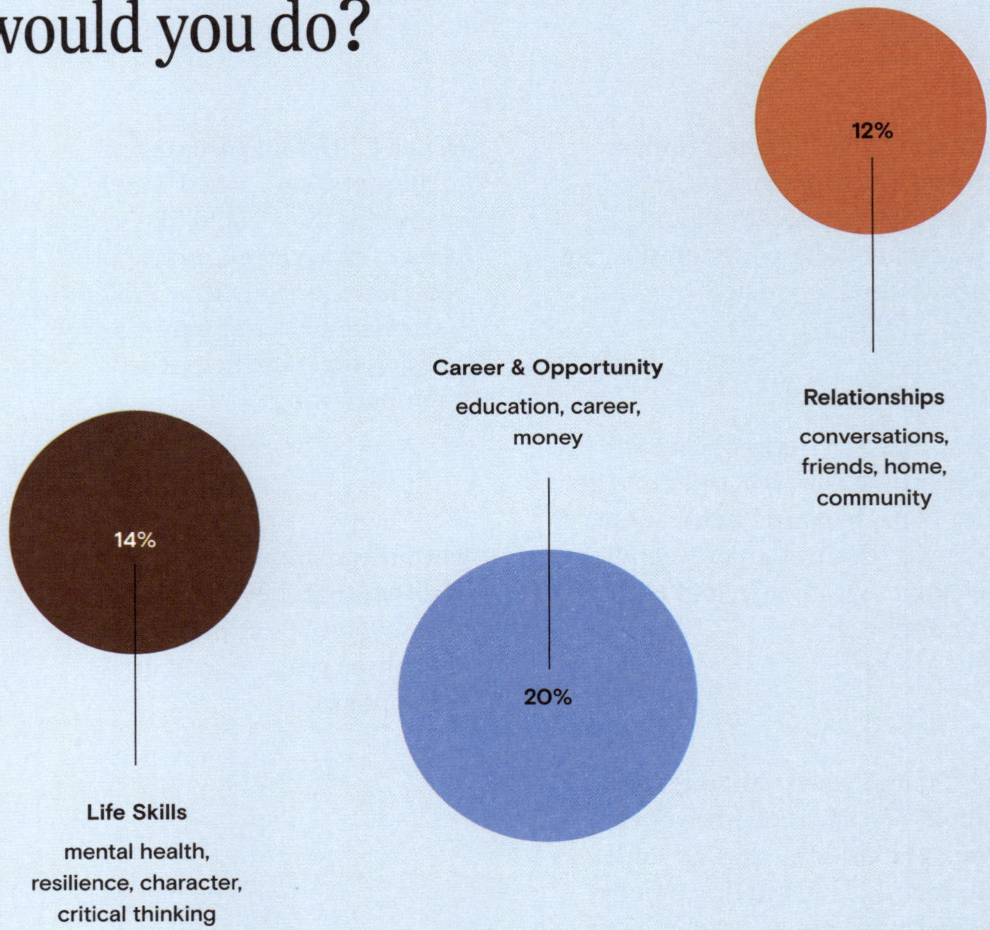

12%

Relationships
conversations, friends, home, community

Career & Opportunity
education, career, money

14%

20%

Life Skills
mental health, resilience, character, critical thinking

n= 500 U.S. parents with kids ages 0–25, June 2021;

Section 04   Open Ended   What Most Parents Aren't Telling You

Safety & Acceptance
violence, hate, bullying,
guns, prejudice

33%

14%

Public Policy
food, environment,
health care, drugs

Other
no hope—
or magic beans

6%

→ When parent responses to the open-ended question were grouped, the majority fell into one of five categories. Of the responses that qualified as "other" most indicated either a hopelessness too deep to imagine a better world, or what we will call a "magic beans" desire for something so spectacular it can't be put into one of the more practical categories below: although, we do think it would be cool if we could give kids the ability to time-travel. This is generally how parents responded.

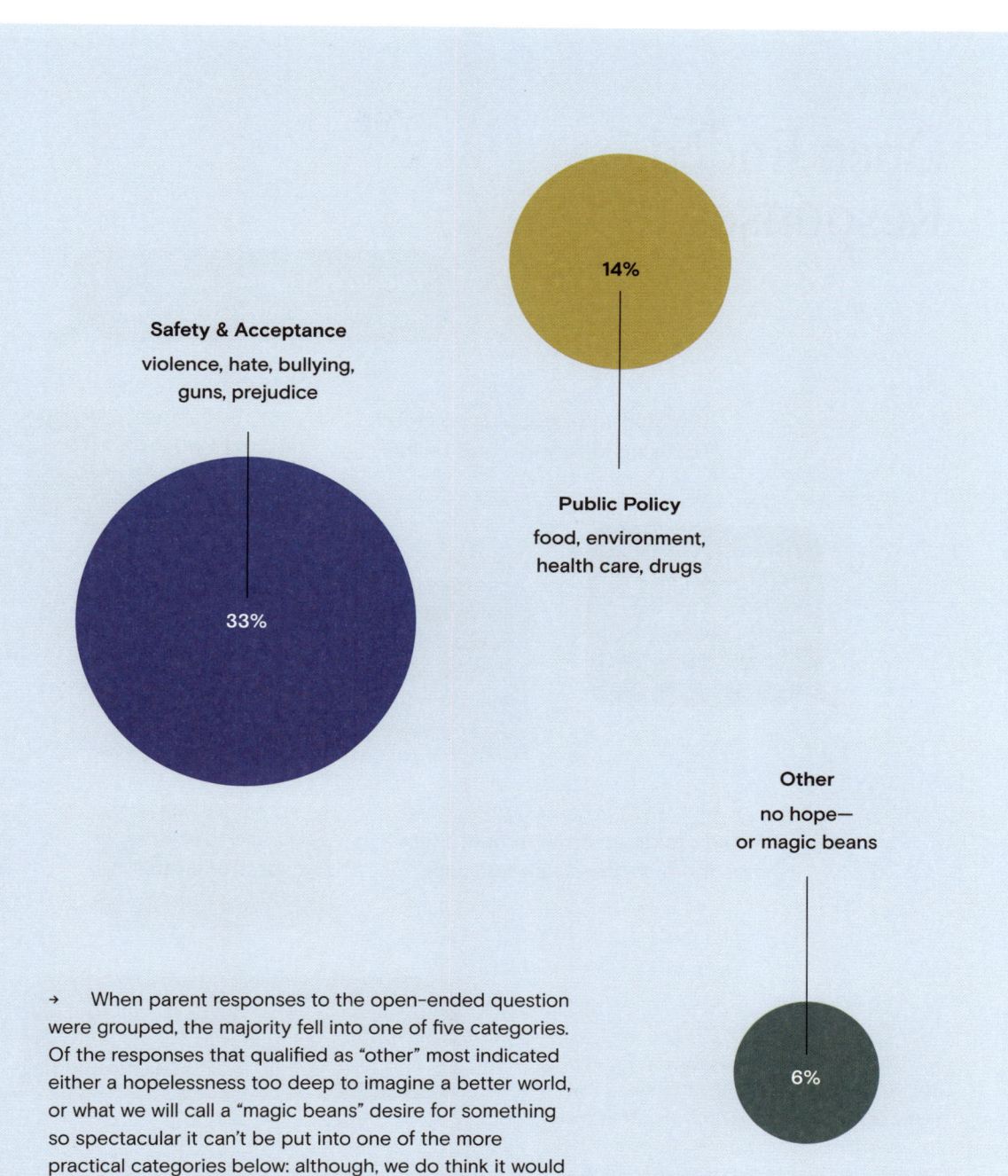

Open Ended Responses

> I would end racism, sexism, and discrimination of all kinds.

> I wish it were possible to stop bullying in schools and online.

> I would want them to know that I will always be there for them.

> I would teach my son the value of self-worth and how to recover from failure.

> I wish more people were educated about difference. My son was born with a clubbed foot and I constantly worry that he will be bullied because people don't understand his condition.

> I would create an environment that helps them succeed academically.

> I would teach my daughter critical thinking skills.

> I would continue to bring awareness to and help eliminate racism as my daughter is multi-racial.

→ Parents indicate they have concerns about their kid's future world in areas that many churches aren't discussing. This raises the question: Is faith connected to a better future? If so, how might ministry leaders speak into the areas people naturally care about for the sake of the next generation?

> I would end poverty.

> I wish there were more resources for college preparation for single parents.

> I wish we could all live more sustainably with less waste and pollution.

> I would make sure he has access to good resources on sex education even if he doesn't feel comfortable talking to me about it.

> I just want to be able to set aside enough money for his future.

> I wish we had access to speech therapy without jumping through so many hoops.

> I wish his mom would be more respectful to his dad who has primary custody.

> I would like to have her father not only accept and acknowledge her, but also want to know her and be a part of her life.

> I wish we had better ways to stop the stigma regarding blind kids.

> I would end hunger.

Section #05
Cultural Distinctions by Race & Ethnicity

→ One-third of U.S. congregations are largely composed of a specific racial or ethnic majority. In a nation that is currently 60% White, non-Hispanic or Latino, many racial and ethnic minorities look for a center of worship that better reflects their cultural distinctives rather than blending with majority culture.

At the same time, multi-ethnic churches and parishes are on the rise and often work hard to reflect the cultural diversity of their community by making stronger efforts for inclusion from the leadership, to the platform, to the congregation as a whole.[29] Ministry leaders in every context need to understand how race and ethnicity impact the experience of those they serve.

Perhaps nowhere are racial and ethnic distinctions more noteworthy than when it comes to family. Though parents of every ethnicity share similar parenting styles, worries, and hopes for their kids' futures, each family is unique and nuanced based on their lived experiences and family history. For ministry leaders who serve a population of parents with a specific racial or ethnic majority, it's important to note where and how these populations may differ from the more general findings of this study.

And, for every ministry leader, it's important to recognize that racial demographic shifts are on the horizon. For young people, they are growing up in a country where diversity is the norm as racial minorities constitute the majority of their cohort. And, as the mosaic of different races, ethnicities, and cultures expand and blend, the look and feel of the total population will continue to shift—the Browning of the United States, the growth of the mixed-race population, and the increase of Asian Americans as the fastest growing single-race U.S. demographic continue to challenge perceptions that the country is Black and White. In fact, data from the 2020 United States Census Bureau projects non-Hispanic White Americans will become the minority demographic by 2045, with anecdotal evidence predicting a majority-minority flip much sooner.[30]

Astute leaders are using population forecasts to signal a closer look at racial and ethnic diversity and how it will impact the future of their church. For those who currently minister in a setting with a specific racial or ethnic majority, it's important to note where and how their families may differ from the more general findings in this study and how that may shift over time as the overall population changes.

In the following pages, we will note the statistically-significant differences among Black, White, Latino, and Asian American parents in our study.[31] A reflection on these findings will follow with some context for how to best interpret and properly respond to the data.

Section 05   Cultural Distinctions   What Most Parents Aren't Telling You

Distinctions for Black Parents

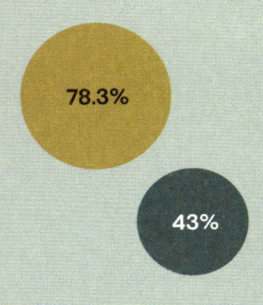

78.3%

43%

→ 78.3% of Black parents say their kids' faith is *important* or *extremely important* compared to 43% of parents of other races and ethnicities.

What Black Parents Want

Like the majority of parents in this generation, Black parents highly value their kids' mental health and character development. But, Black parents value educational achievement for their kids higher than access to opportunities. Another noteworthy distinction among Black parents is the level of importance they give to their kids' faith. Black parents elevate the importance of their kids' faith higher than any other ethnicity by 27%.

What Black Parents Fear

Black parents, on average, worry more than any other racial demographic. When asked to qualify what extent they worry about certain areas in their kids' lives, Black parents cite specifically higher worries than other ethnicities in the areas of faith, racism, influence of peers, and busyness and exhaustion. Black parents' worries about faith may not come as a surprise given the significantly higher value they place on their kids' faith. But, many Black parents (45%) also say they worry often or all the time about racism, making it their second-highest concern.

What Black Parents Feel

Black parents value community, which directly impacts the way they feel about themselves. As compared to other racial and ethnic groups, Black parents describe themselves as more *connected*. And, Black parents say they feel more *supported* than other groups in the areas of faith (+20%), sexual integrity (+15%) and responsible use of technology (+15%). Black parents also report 10% greater support than other groups in the areas of community involvement, career readiness, college preparation, healthy mentors, and access to resources. One notable distinction is that while Black parents feel more supported in the area of healthy mentors for their kids, 35% of Black parents (more than any other group) say they want more mentoring adults invested in their kids' success.

Where Black Parents Find Help

When it comes to finding help for their parenting, Black parents are more likely than other groups to consult their extended family, ex-partner, or church. And Black parents are less likely to search for parenting help online or through social platforms like Facebook.

Perhaps the most consistent distinction for Black parents is their elevated value of faith, worry about faith, feelings of support for faith, and tendency to look to their church for help with parenting. Leaders working with Black families may feel additional pressure to stay up-to-date on parenting topics in order to meet the needs of Black parents. And they may also have far greater opportunities to encourage and support Black parents in their parenting journey.

Black Parents Differ in Their Fears

The percent of parents who say they worry *often* or *all the time* about each concern.

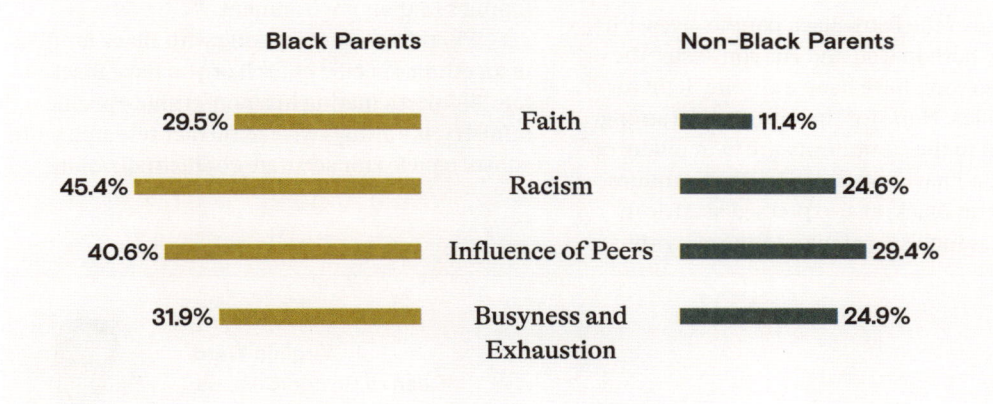

Black Parents	Concern	Non-Black Parents
29.5%	Faith	11.4%
45.4%	Racism	24.6%
40.6%	Influence of Peers	29.4%
31.9%	Busyness and Exhaustion	24.9%

n = 1,464 U.S. parents with kids 0–25, June 2021

Reflections About
Black Parents

The fondest memories of my childhood and teen years are rooted in the Black church. My faith development was important to my parents, and they relied on the church for holistic support of our family. We were not alone. The local church served many other Black families in our community with a myriad of resources including mentoring, financial assistance, and tutoring.

My work with Black families over the years proved to be very communal, often with reciprocal support to my family as well. Parents from single and two-parent homes welcomed the additional support for their children and became the support for other households. It was understood that each parent would make a deposit into another and could expect a withdrawal when needed.

As a daughter of a Caribbean and African American family, it is no surprise to me that Black families elevate the importance of faith in the lives of their children more than any other ethnic group. Faith has traditionally been front and center in the lives of many parents who desire to pass their faith on to their children. The song, *We've Come This Far by Faith*, written by Albert A. Goodson (an African American), continues to be a mantra for Black families.

> We've come this far by faith,
> Leaning on the Lord,
> Trusting in His holy Word
> He has never failed me yet.

In spite of the fears Black parents live with constantly, faith in God and His son Jesus, the suffering servant, have been a guiding light for Black families. Hope for the future and a strong connection to the community are twin pillars of support that I have witnessed in Black families.

The term Black, also expressed as African American, is inclusive of many cultures within the African diaspora such as African, Caribbean, Afro-Latina, and bi-racial. There is a phrase that is attributed to an old African Proverb: It takes a village to raise a child. The practice of "village raising" is a common understanding within the Black community with its roots coming from African traditions. Elders were respected as they provided wisdom and history through oral and written avenues.

Racism has been, and continues to be, a major fear for Black families in the West more than other ethnicities. While many conversations focus on racism directly, the elevated level of worry Black parents demonstrate for other sources of concern like the influence of peers, and busyness and exhaustion, are also real indicators of the same, larger societal problems. It's crucial for church leaders to be aware of these issues when ministering to Black families.

Like all families, Black families share a concern for their kids' academic success and character development. And Black parents expect ministry leaders to take these into account in order to provide a well-rounded support system.

This data is a snapshot of a broad spectrum of Black families in the West. It should be used as an indicator of what parents want, need, fear, and hope for in their children. As a limited snapshot, leaders should exercise caution to avoid over generalizing this data for the spectrum of Black families in their environment.

Whether you are working with Black families in an ethnic specific church or you have Black families participating in a non-ethnic-specific ministry, it's always wise to further research your constituencies for accurate contextualization.

Virginia Ward
Dean of Boston Campus,
Gordon Conwell Theological Seminary

Distinctions for White Parents

What White Parents Want

White parents, like all parents, value their kids' mental health, character development, and access to opportunities. A noteworthy distinction among White parents, however, is the comparatively low importance they assign to their kids' faith. Only 27% of White parents say their kids' faith development is *important* to *extremely important*. White parents prioritize the importance of their kids' faith lower than any other ethnicity by 24%.

What White Parents Fear

White parents worry less than parents of different races and ethnicities. On average, 24.1% of White parents say they worry often or all the time about the concerns listed in this study. This compares to 30% of non-White parents who say the same. White parents specifically report lower levels of concern for their kids' faith, sexual behavior, drug and alcohol use, violence and weapons, suicide, racism, and busyness and exhaustion.

What White Parents Feel

As compared to other racial and ethnic groups, White parents describe themselves as *supported* (- 4.3%) and *connected* (- 8.4%) less often than other parents. White parents also describe themselves as *alone*, *inadequate*, and *judged* more often than other parents. Both White and Asian parents report feeling lower levels of support than Black and Hispanic parents generally. And White parents report the lowest levels of support in the areas of healthy mentors, college preparation, career readiness, access to opportunities, physical exercise, faith development, and community involvement.

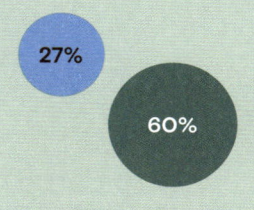

→ 27% of White parents say their kids' faith is *important* or *extremely important* compared to 60% of parents of other races and ethnicities.

Where White Parents Find Help

When it comes to finding help for their parenting, White parents are more likely to consult their spouse/partner or friends/neighbors than parents of any other group. And White parents also look for parenting help through internet searches and online communities more often than parents of other race or ethnic groups. More than 65% of White parents say they would like more family experiences to attend with their kids, more than parents of any other race or ethnicity.

White Parents Differ in Their Fears

The percent of parents who say they worry *often* or *all the time* about each concern.

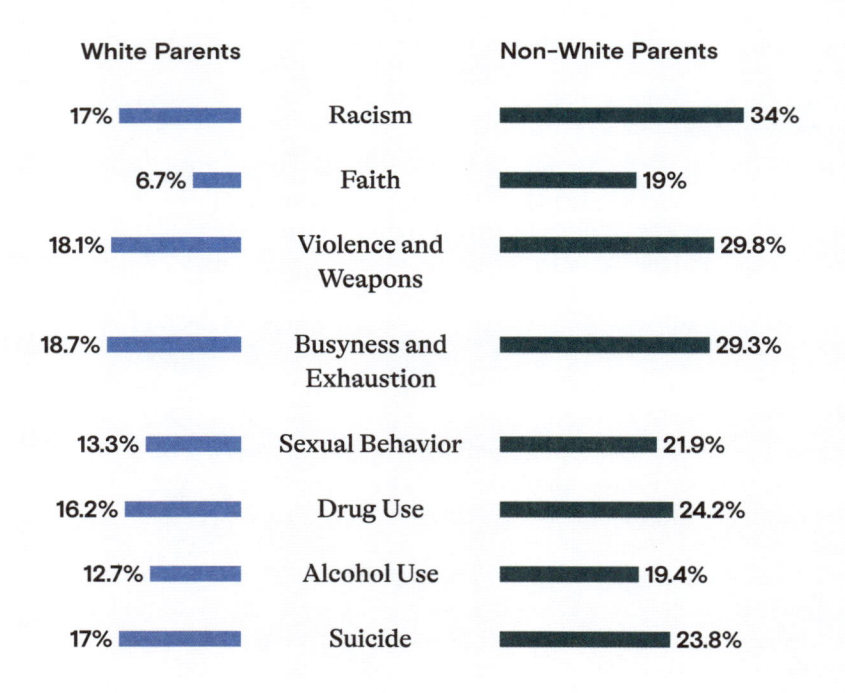

White Parents		Non-White Parents
17%	Racism	34%
6.7%	Faith	19%
18.1%	Violence and Weapons	29.8%
18.7%	Busyness and Exhaustion	29.3%
13.3%	Sexual Behavior	21.9%
16.2%	Drug Use	24.2%
12.7%	Alcohol Use	19.4%
17%	Suicide	23.8%

n = 1,464 U.S. parents with kids 0–25, June 2021

Reflections About
White Parents

When you think about the everyday experiences of White parents, you may picture minivans, Starbucks lattes, and golf clubs. But you'd be missing a huge portion of White parent experiences—ones where parents feel constant pressure to be everything their kids need, where the "keeping up with the Jones" (or Kardashians) is a never ending striving, and where the main feeling expressed by their community (and maybe even their church) is *pressure*.

Our research illuminates that White parents describe themselves as *alone*, *inadequate*, and *judged* more often than parents of any other ethnicity. Our research also shows that White parents feel lower levels of support than Black and Asian parents.

These findings make sense in the context of an individualized, success-driven, comparative culture. White parents are raised to pride themselves on their ability to parent well, or at least to give the impression of parenting well. To ask for help, especially in any kind of real or substantive way, might make a White parent feel like a failure. This pressure on individual success tends to leave both parents and kids feeling more isolated and stressed.

At the same time, White parents worry *less* than parents of different races and ethnicities. White parents specifically report lower levels of concern for their kids' sexual behavior, drug and alcohol use, violence and weapons, suicide, racism, and busyness and exhaustion.

But the one finding in our research that rattles me most (and should rattle you) is that White parents prioritize the importance of their kids' faith lower than any other ethnicity by 24%.

What is it about a high performance culture that minimizes the values of community and faith? As a leader who has worked in White churches for most of my life, I'm bothered by the way so many families seem to be leaving church behind as they strive to measure up to what seems like an impossible standard.

Beneath the "all I need are Jesus and coffee" kitchen signs or #raisethemup social media posts, do White parents feel like instilling faith is another task to make sure they complete, or a life they can genuinely live—one that may include mistakes.

Maybe our challenge as ministry leaders is to help parents understand that constantly trying to measure up to an ideal image may set them up to be disillusioned when life doesn't live up to the picture they had for their family. Instead, we should invite them into a bigger story mindset where they trust that God will keep writing His story of grace in their lives, regardless.

Parenting is difficult. It is by far the hardest thing I have ever done. I would never minimize the strains, tensions, heartbreak, and realities of any parent's story. Instead, what if we create churches that feel safe enough for all parents to be exactly who they are, and still know they can belong.

Stuart Hall
Director of Student Leadership, Orange

Distinctions for Asian Parents

What Asian Parents Want

Like the majority of parents in this generation, Asian parents highly value their kids' mental health, character development, and access to opportunities. But more Asian parents than Black or Latino parents say their kids' mental health is *important* or *extremely important*. And, more Asian parents rate the development of their kids' character as *important* or *extremely important* than all other racial and ethnic groups. 96.5% of Asian parents say both mental health and character development are the most important things they want for their kids.

What Asian Parents Fear

Asian parents worry less than Black or Latino parents. 24.3% of Asian parents report worrying *often* or *all of the time* about the concerns listed in this study. This compares to 30% of non-Asian parents who say the same. Asian parents specifically report the lowest level of concern for their kids' anxiety, depression, technology influence, being bullied by other kids, body image, peer influence, good eating habits/nutrition, and getting enough sleep. However, Asian parents report worrying more than White or Latino parents about their children's busyness and exhaustion.

What Asian Parents Feel

As compared to other racial and ethnic groups, Asian parents describe themselves as *aware* more often than Black, Latino, and White parents (+5.6%). And Asian parents are less likely than other parents to describe themselves as *present/responsive*, *nurturing*, *alone*, *distracted*, *judged*, and *lazy*. As compared to Black, White, and Latino parents, fewer Asian parents (-10%) feel they know more about their kids than the other adult influencers in their kids' life.

Asian parents report feeling lower levels of support than any other racial or ethnic group. 31.2% of Asian parents say they feel *supported* or *well-supported* in all areas of parenting. This compares to 38.9% of non-Asian parents who would say the same. Asian parents report the lowest levels of support in the areas of access to resources, educational achievement, use of technology, friendship with my kid, mental health, character development, strong friendships, sexual integrity, balanced nutrition, and extended family connections.

Where Asian Parents Find Help

Like all parents, the majority of Asian parents are most likely to consult a spouse or partner for parenting help. But Asian parents are more likely to consult online sources for parenting advice before asking for help from friends/neighbors or their extended family. In fact, fewer Asian parents (-11.7%) than Black, Latino, or White parents say they have consulted their extended family for help with their parenting. Asian parents say preschool is more helpful to their family than parents in other race or ethnicity groups. And Asian parents report the highest level of church attendance, saying they attend church weekly (+7.6%) more than Black, White, and Latino parents.

Like all parents, Asian parents (55.8%) want more family experiences they can attend together. But, Asian parents are more likely than other parents to say they would like more practical training (35.4%) to help prioritize parenting efforts.

Asian Parents Differ in Their Fears

The percent of parents who say they worry *often* or *all the time* about each concern.

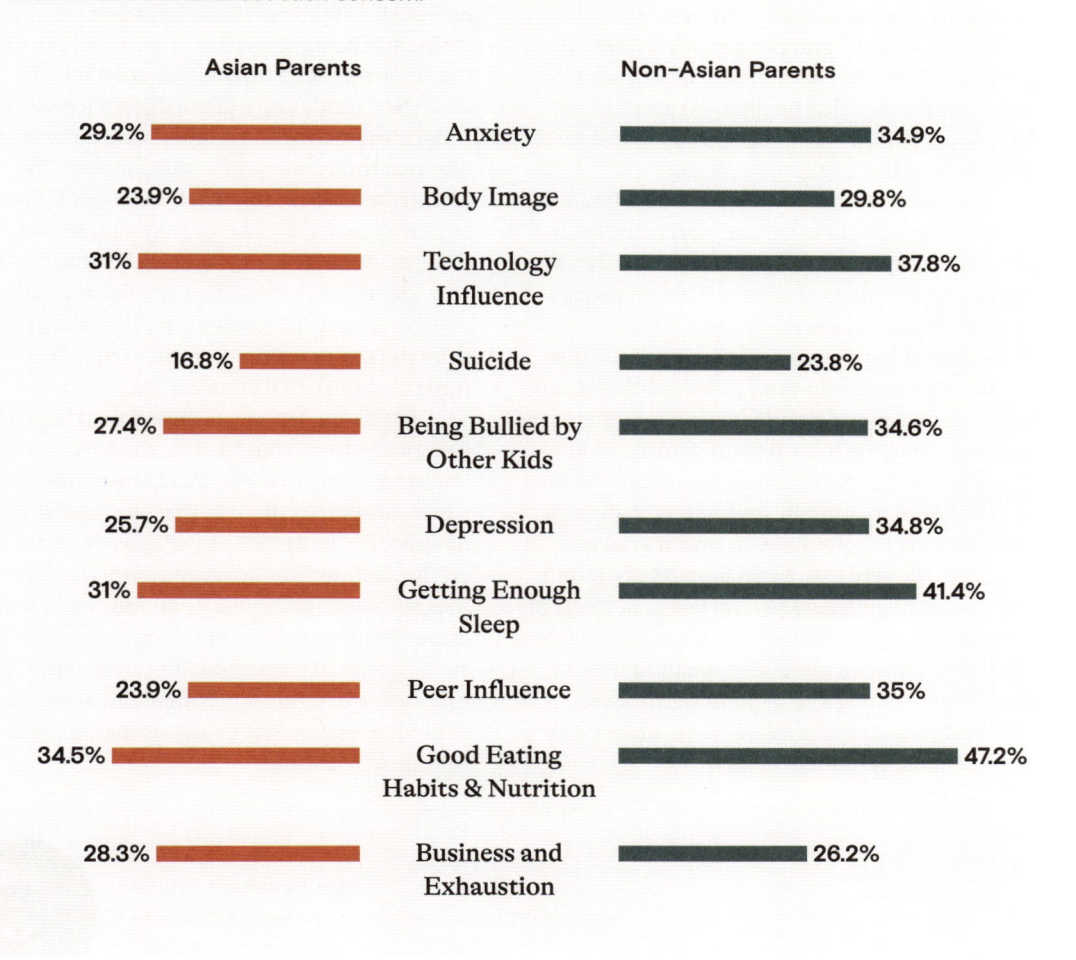

Asian Parents		Non-Asian Parents
29.2%	Anxiety	34.9%
23.9%	Body Image	29.8%
31%	Technology Influence	37.8%
16.8%	Suicide	23.8%
27.4%	Being Bullied by Other Kids	34.6%
25.7%	Depression	34.8%
31%	Getting Enough Sleep	41.4%
23.9%	Peer Influence	35%
34.5%	Good Eating Habits & Nutrition	47.2%
28.3%	Business and Exhaustion	26.2%

n = 1,464 U.S. parents with kids 0–25, June 2021

Reflections About
Asian Parents

Family is central to all communities, but Asian Americans (especially those who are foreign-born) tend to place greater importance on parenting and marriage than the general population. Asian Americans (especially mothers) often go to great lengths in the sacrifices they make for their children. And for many, the success of their children defines their own sense of success.

Asian cultures are generally more collectivist in orientation. So, many Asian Americans (especially those who are closer to their ethnic heritage) are enculturated to lift instead of add burdens to others—and possess what Koreans would call 눈치 ("noonchi"), which is an acute social awareness. This heightened awareness drives people from Asian backgrounds to actively avoid feeling like a burden to others.

For these reasons, Asian parents often fail to reach out for help with their parenting both because it may make them feel like a burden as well as elicit feelings of shame. This is perhaps why Asian parents are more likely to feel unsupported than other racial groups, and also less likely to seek help from people outside their family and friends, turning instead to impersonal resources (like the internet and books).

Like most parents, Asian Americans want their children to flourish, and a significant aspect of flourishing is belonging. In multiracial and multicultural settings, Asian parents often find themselves negotiating several layers of internal and cultural conflicts that lead them to struggle in silence. This can often lead Asian American parents to feel invisible in plain sight. Asian Americans won't often ask for help, unless it is offered, and offered repeatedly.

One of the key findings of this report suggests that mental health is important for Asian American families. Historically, there has been widespread stigma against seeking mental health support within the Asian American community. But things may be changing. During the pandemic, it was reported that Asian Americans experienced the greatest mental health challenges of any racial group. Add to this the reports that during the pandemic, 80% of Asian American teens recorded bullying either in person or online, half of all Asian Americans experienced a racist incident, and 32% of Asian Americans felt afraid that they might be threatened or attacked.

The Church can make a difference. Asian Americans are the most religiously diverse racial group in the country, of whom around 37% identify as Christian/Catholic. (78% of Filipinos, 56% of Koreans, 35% of Vietnamese, 32% of Chinese Americans, and 31% of Japanese). Those who identify as evangelical have historically had a high commitment to their faith, yet, it appears to be the group declining most among the Asian American Christian community.

For Asian American Christians, the Asian American church has historically served as a house of worship as well as a community center, which supported them as they learned how to navigate life in the U.S. As religiosity seems to be on the decline among many groups, including the Asian American Christian community, it will be important for all churches to find ways that ensure a deep sense of belonging, meet the needs of Asian Americans in culturally competent ways, and be willing to respond to the issues that impact Asian American families.

Pastor Raymond Chang
President, Asian American Christian Collaborative
Campus Minister, Wheaton College

Distinctions for Latino Parents

What Latino Parents Want

Like the majority of parents in this generation, Latino parents highly value their kids' mental health and access to opportunities. But Latino parents value educational achievement for their kids higher than character development. Still, greater than 90% of Latino parents say character development, along with access to resources and physical exercise are *important* or *extremely important* for their kids.

Latino parents elevate the importance of their friendship with their kids higher than any other ethnicity. They also prioritize the value of strong friendships for their kids higher than Black or Asian parents, further signaling a strong value for building and maintaining relationships.

What Latino Parents Fear

Latino parents worry more often than White or Asian parents, and 31.9% of Latino parents say they worry *often* or *all the time* about the concerns listed in this study. Latino parents specifically report higher levels of concern for their kids' anxiety, depression, the influence of technology, alcohol consumption, being bullied by other kids, suicide, and getting enough sleep. Of these concerns, Latino parents worry about their kids' mental health is most notable. More Latino parents worry about suicide than parents of any other race or ethnic group.

What Latino Parents Feel

More than half of Latino parents say they know their kids better than other adults in their kids' life. And, as compared to other racial and ethnic groups, Latino parents describe themselves as *confident* more often than Black, Asian, and White parents (+7.2%).

Latino parents also describe themselves as *confused* more often than parents of other ethnicities and described themselves as *capable* less often than parents of other groups.

When it comes to feeling supported, Latino parents say they feel higher levels of support in the areas of character development (+3.2%), access to opportunities (+9.5), and strong friendships (+10.3%) compared to White, Black, and Asian parents.

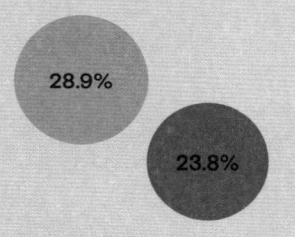

→ 28.9% of Latino parents say they worry about suicide *often* or *all of the time* compared to 23.8% of parents of other races and ethnicities.

Where Latino Parents Find Help

Latino parents are more likely than White or Asian parents to consult sources of help for parenting. Like all parents, Latino parents are most likely to consult a spouse/partner for parenting help. But, compared to Black, White, and Asian parents, Latino parents are more likely to consult YouTube (+5.8%), books (+5.9%), podcasts (+5.4%), and mobile apps (+8.9%) as well.

Like all parents, Latino parents (54.8%) want more family experiences they can attend together. But, Latino parents are more likely than other parents to say they would like more resources to understand their kids at every phase (47.6%).

Latino Parents Differ in Their Fears

The percent of parents who say they worry *often* or *all the time* about each concern.

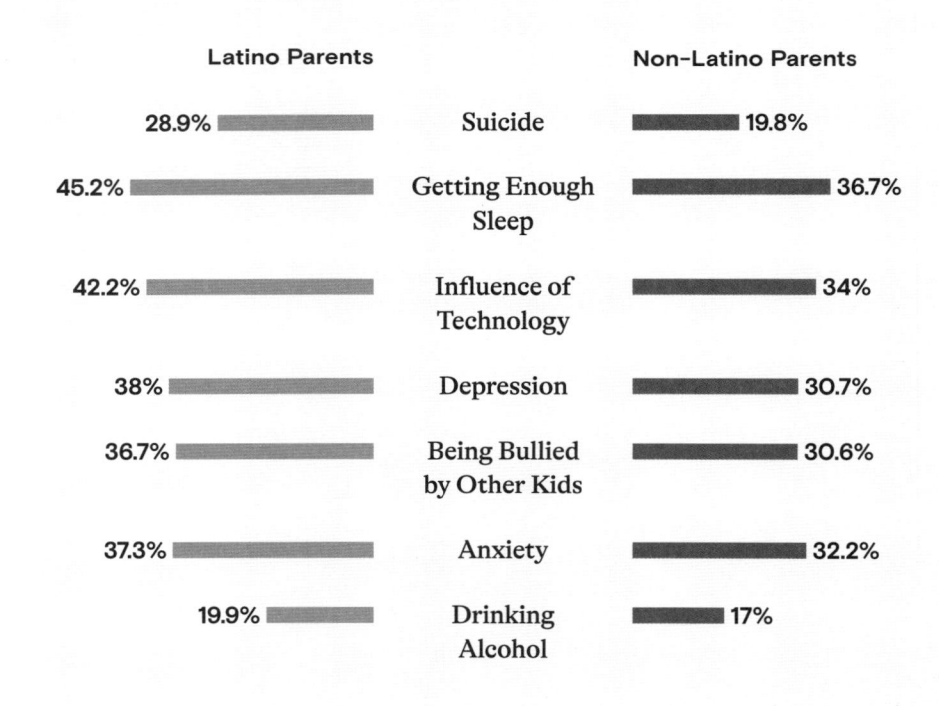

Latino Parents	Concern	Non-Latino Parents
28.9%	Suicide	19.8%
45.2%	Getting Enough Sleep	36.7%
42.2%	Influence of Technology	34%
38%	Depression	30.7%
36.7%	Being Bullied by Other Kids	30.6%
37.3%	Anxiety	32.2%
19.9%	Drinking Alcohol	17%

n = 1,464 U.S. parents with kids 0-25, June 2021

Reflections About
U.S. Latino Parents

To simplify and summarize the differences between Hispanic parents and others, Hispanic parents place more emphasis on relationship with their children, and yet, they feel both more eager for them to succeed and more worried about their well-being. They also are hungrier to find whatever resources they can that will help.

These differences are not surprising for those of us who live and work primarily in Hispanic communities. Research consistently supports that Hispanic cultures are relational, collective, and place a very high value on family.[32] In our study at Centro Latino of Latinx millennials, we learned that sons and daughters are in general more connected to their parents and grandparents than in the mainstream culture. The emphasis on family relationship goes both ways. Anyone who wants to help Hispanic parents needs to recognize not only the importance of family but also a different definition of family. Family in the Hispanic context is extended family—cousins, aunts and uncles, grandparents, godparents. All of these sources of help and support matter to Hispanic parents. Outside resources are also welcome but should be offered in a way that respects indigenous, existing resources. The family connections of Hispanics are a great example and potential positive influence for mainstream U.S. culture at this moment in history.

The desire for children to achieve and the determination to take advantage of new resources are classic aspects of immigrant communities in general. Roughly 45% of the Hispanics in the United States are foreign-born. Immigration from Latin America is ongoing. Most Hispanics have relatives and acquaintances who are migrants even if they themselves are citizens. Immigrants see the new society as a place of both new threats and new opportunities. They want their children to take advantage of all of the new opportunities, and they themselves want access to any new resources that could help them in their parenting. At the same time, they are more worried about the health and lives of their children. Living with a threat for a long period of time can easily create a level of acceptance, if not comfort. The new encounter with a threat naturally sparks a higher level of fear and anxiety.

Lastly, it is also important to note that Hispanics, particularly Hispanic immigrants, are more likely to have faith than the average American. Roughly 95% of Latin Americans identify as Christians, and in Latin America, non-Catholic Christian churches are growing three times as quickly as the Catholic Church.[33] Immigrants from Latin America often bring a vibrant faith with them across the border. The question is not whether they believe; it is what they believe. I would imagine that the data on Christian families vs. secular families would also be relevant to the particular needs of Hispanic parents. Faith is such a ground of being in Latin America that parents may assume that character development includes faith development, and therefore not state it explicitly. Yet, offering opportunities for educational achievement and character development that include faith development would tend to be welcomed, even by people without an explicit commitment to Christian discipleship.

Rev. Dr. Alexia Salvatierra
Dean of the Centro Latino, Fuller Theological Seminary
Assistant Professor of Integral Mission and Global Transformation

What's something someone could have done for your parent when you were growing up that would have helped them be a better parent?

> Be their friend.
> —*Orange County, CA*

> My single mother had financial support from the church to send us (three girls) to summer camp, but rarely supported her in the day-to-day life of being a single mom. Me and my siblings went hungry many nights and spent many days alone because she was working so hard. I wish someone would have noticed. —*Pittsburgh, PA*

> My parents would have been better parents if people in the church would have called and just checked in. My family was a huge part of church and then stepped away. No one ever checked on us. —*Kansas City, KS*

> As immigrants, my parents may have benefited from other parents explaining cultural norms that weren't easily understood by them. May have helped navigate conversations between them and their children. —*Columbus, OH*

> I am the product of a broken marriage that ended officially when I was 5. If someone (besides family) would have reached out to her and invited her to dinner, church, just some companionship as she struggled to raise me on a limited income, I think she may have come out of the depression she was in for awhile after. She eventually got there (and found happiness and remarried) but it was a tough 4 years. —*Charlotte, NC*

> To let my single mom know she wasn't any less than the "intact" families. —*Charlotte, NC*

> I am a Pastor's kid and I wish someone would have helped my parents by not condemning my mom because she couldn't do as much as she wanted to at church. She was working a full-time job to support our family and taking care of us while my Dad was out doing ministry. —*Lancaster, PA*

> My parents took in three kids who were our neighbors when their mom died. My parents were too tired to go to church. They needed help at home. They needed resources and people to donate their time. —*Pittsburgh, PA*

> Meet her (my mom) where she was instead of expecting her to be someone she wasn't or couldn't be. —*Austin, TX*

> Someone could have surrounded my parents in love and truth when they failed. Instead, they felt isolated and judged, and unwelcome. —*Indianapolis, IN*

Since my dad was a single parent, creating community would have helped my dad because he had no support system. The church left him alone when times were tough. —*Orange County, CA*

Something someone could have done to help my mom parent her kids - show up. Raised by a single working mom, sometimes my brother and I needed more help than she could give. We needed healthy people to help fill the void, bring us meals, drive us places, just help. —*Indianapolis, IN*

My dad was hard of hearing, I am hard of hearing, and my sister had special needs. We couldn't always be at church together as a family, finances were tight and my parents often went without. I wish people had seen my Dad's isolation not as standoffish, but instead had noticed his incredible leadership skills. And, I wish my mother had been equipped to be a female leader in the church just like she was at home. —*Columbus, OH*

Listen —*Chicago, IL*

I don't know if church leaders actually knew me or my name. My mom mostly spoke another language so I'm not sure if they ever were able to have a conversation about me. —*Austin, TX*

I didn't grow up in church. My parents divorced when I was very young and my parents (separately) struggled with addiction and mental illness. I think they always felt ashamed to approach the Church or people in the church because they weren't willing to meet them where they were. Something that could have helped our family win would have been the Church taking time to empower school teachers in their church to have conversations with kids like me. —*Austin, TX*

I was adopted from Europe when I was 2. I would have loved other adoptive parents to walk alongside of mine and give them advice and wisdom. We know so much more about adoption now, but it was never celebrated in my life and that is a huge loss I think. —*Dallas, TX*

It would have helped if my mom knew she wasn't going to be judged for her past abuser which led to her drinking problem. If the church would have been willing to accept all of her and not feel uncomfortable when she came into the church, maybe she would have known God loved her and turned to a church family instead of alcohol. I ran to God by getting on a church bus that came to *me*, which I wish it would have come for *her*. —*Dallas, TX*

To have let my mom know that being divorced didn't mean that she was an outcast or failure in parenting. —*Columbus, OH*

Letting them know they are doing a good job and that it's ok to not always know the answer... every single kid is unique and requires a different set of boundaries. —*Seattle, WA*

→ With over 500 honest and personal responses, there were many that stood out. These are only a few.

Section #06
Notable Distinctions by Family Structure

→ The structure and composition of U.S. families is diversifying year after year. People are waiting longer to get married, and fewer people are deciding to have children. Cohabitating couples now compose 12% of coupled households, and the number of families with biological children under eighteen has declined by 5% over the past ten years. Today, one-third of children living in the United States live in a single-parent household. On average, more than half of young adults eighteen to twenty-four still live with their parents. The number of grandparent-as-primary-caregiver households is on the rise, and one out of every 25 families with children in the U.S. includes an adopted child. The family unit isn't changing. It's already changed.

Though parents in every family structure share similar parenting styles, worries, and hopes for their kids' futures, each family is unique and nuanced based on their lived experiences and family history. Leaders who want to truly engage families, and serve parents well, must begin by understanding what it means to be *family* in a variety of contexts.

As we look into the distinctive data around various family structure, it's important to remember that many categories overlap. Some single parents are raising adopted kids. Some blended families are also same-sex couples. That's not to mention that family structure is also set against the backdrop of other distinctions like income, gender, race, and ethnicity.

No one snapshot can give the full context for any family, which may be why so many Christian parents say their church has trouble supporting their parenting. This study found that 51% of parents have concerns about how their pastor understands the realities of their family life. Given the variety of family dynamics, it's impossible for any leader to have personal experience in every category. Personal experience often informs our assumptions about parenting and family in general, and sometimes, what may have been true for us just isn't as true for everyone.

In the following pages, we will note the areas of this study that showed statistically significant differences between the general findings and the specific findings for single-parents, foster and adoptive parents, blended family parents, and same-sex couple parents.

Distinctions for Single Parents

What Single Parents Want
Single parents do not differ substantially from other parents in the area of parenting values. Like most parents, the majority of single parents value mental health, access to opportunities, and character development as *important* or *extremely important*. Single parents do differ from the general population of parents by placing a higher level of importance on access to resources, healthy mentors, and technological responsibility. By comparison, 89.3% of single parents and 86.2% of HS* parents say healthy mentors are *important* or *extremely important*. Single parents also differ from the general population of parents by placing a lower level of importance on college preparation and faith development.

→ To simplify reporting, we will use an abbreviated HS to denote the family structure of a two parent caregiver heterosexual parent.

35%

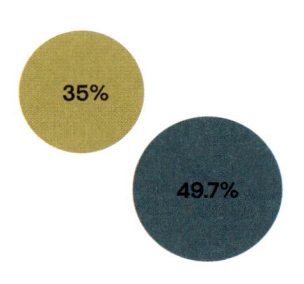

49.7%

→ Only 35% of single parents as compared to 49.7% of two-caregiver, heterosexual parents say faith is *important* or *extremely important* for their kids.

What Single Parents Fear

Single parents worry more than non-single parents about the things that might harm their kids' future. In fact, in the list of 17 potential parenting concerns included in this study, nutrition is the only concern single parents worry about less than the general population. Single parents worry significantly more than the general population of parents about their kids in the areas of depression, sexual behavior, drug use, violence and weapons, and getting enough sleep. Interestingly, even though single parents rated faith less important than HS parents, 15.3% of single parents as compared to 9.7% of HS parents, say they worry *often* or *all of the time* about their kids' faith.

What Single Parents Feel

When asked to select adjectives that describe their parenting, single parents, like all parents, select more positive adjectives than negative. Single parents do not differ from the general population of parents in their top three responses: capable, nurturing, and present/responsive, but there are some differences. Single parents are more likely than the general population of parents to say they are alone, judged, and inadequate. And, single parents are less likely than the general population of parents to say they are nurturing, present/responsive, or connected. By comparison, 15.8% of single parents describe themselves as alone, as compared to 5.3% of HS parents.

Where Single Parents Go for Help

When it comes to finding help for their parenting, single parents differ most in the number who have consulted an ex-partner or current spouse/partner for parenting help. But single parents also report having consulted online videos, podcasts, mobile apps, community centers, and churches more than the general population of parents. By contrast, a higher percent of single parents (24.6%) than heterosexual couples (16.3%), same-sex couples (20%), or parents of blended families (22.9%) say they have consulted a church for parenting help. Like all parents, more than half of single parents say they would like more experiences to attend together with their kid. But a greater percentage of single parents (27.1%) than HS parents (25.8%) also say they would like more mentoring adults for their kids.

Distinctions for Foster and Adoptive Parents

There are many, widely varied experiences of what it means to be a foster or adoptive parent. The best way to understand more about the unique landscape of these experiences is like anything else. Discover through experience, relationships, and with an ongoing posture of curiosity to learn more. In order to draw statistically significant findings, this study combined parents raising young people in either a foster or adoption context.

What Foster and Adoptive Parents Want

Like all parents, foster and adoptive parents value mental health and character development as *important* or *extremely important* more often than any other parenting value presented in this study. But unlike all parents, foster and adoptive parents rate a majority of parenting values lower than biological parents. Foster and adoptive parents rate only three parenting values as *important* or *extremely important* more often than biological parents: friendship with my kid, faith, and community involvement.

What Foster and Adoptive Parents Fear

On average foster and adoptive parents worry more frequently than parents with biological kids. In fact, foster and adoptive parents worry more often than other parents about all seventeen potential parenting concerns in this study. The sources of concern that differed most between the two groups were: anxiety, use of technology, being bullied by other kids, alcohol, violence, busyness and exhaustion.

What Foster and Adoptive Parents Feel

Foster and adoptive parents, like all parents, described themselves as *capable*, *engaged*, and *connected* with no real difference. But unlike parents with biological kids, more foster and adoptive parents described themselves as present/responsive (+5.6%), confident (+3.7), and lazy (+5.4). Foster and adoptive parents were less likely than other parents to describe themselves as nurturing (-9.3), aware (-5.5), or judged (-4.5). Like all parents, foster and adoptive parents were nearly three times as likely to describe themselves using a positive adjective as they were to select one of the negative words.

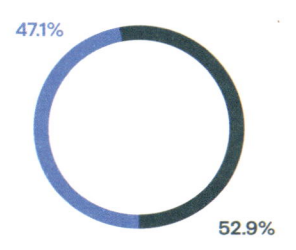

47.1%

52.9%

→ Nearly half (47.1%) of all foster and adoptive parents in the general population say their kids' faith is *important* or *extremely important*.

Where Foster and Adoptive Parents Go for Help

One of the most notable distinctions for foster and adoptive parents is their desire for resources and support. Foster and adoptive parents were on average 10% more likely to consult resources than biological parents. Specifically, foster and adoptive parents were more likely to seek out support from online videos, internet searches, community centers, or a church. Compared to 18.6% of biological parents, 37.3% of foster and adoptive parents say they have consulted a church for parenting help.

Foster and adoptive parents also differed in what resources they wanted. Similar to biological parents, foster and adoptive parents say they want more family experiences to connect with their children. But, 57.1% of foster and adoptive parents also say they want more mentoring adults and practical training to help them prioritize their parenting efforts.

Distinctions for Blended-Family Parents

→ To simplify reporting, we will use an abbreviated BF to denote blended family parents and caregivers.

Blended family experiences come in many different unique combinations of his, hers, theirs, and others. While some blended families have less in common with each other than they might with another sub-group, it's still worth exploring how parents in a blended family context differ from the general findings of this study.

What Blended-Family Parents Want

The majority of BF parents, like all parents, value mental health, access to opportunities, and character development as *important* or *extremely important*. But, by comparison, BF parents rate the majority of parenting values lower than the general population of parents. The only values BF parents rate *important* or *extremely important* more often than the general population are healthy mentors, career readiness, and strong friendships.

What Blended-Family Parents Fear

BF parents worry more than the general population of parents about things that could negatively impact their kids' future. In fact, from the list of seventeen potential parent concerns, BF parents only worry less than the general population of parents in two areas: faith and violence/

weapons. By way of contrast, BF parents worry significantly more than the general population in the areas of anxiety, depression, sexual behavior, use of technology, body image, influence of peers, and getting enough sleep. BF parents worry more than parents in any other family structure about their kids' potential struggles with body image and the influence of peers.

What Blended-Family Parents Feel

Like all parents, the top three adjectives BF parents select to describe themselves are capable, nurturing, and present/responsive. However, BF parents are more likely to describe themselves with negative adjectives, and less likely to select positive adjectives than parents from any other family structure. BF parents are specifically more likely to say they feel judged and inadequate, and less likely to say they feel nurturing, engaged, or supported than the general population. By way of contrast, twice as many BF parents (18.9%) say they feel judged, as compared to the general population (9.4%).

Where Blended-Family Parents Go for Help

BF parents are more likely than single parents, or parents generally, to say they have consulted sources for help with their parenting. BF parents' top source for parenting help is their spouse/partner. BF parents are more likely than the general population of parents to reach out for help with their parenting from every potential source listed in this study other than church. BF parents specifically say they consult the internet, friends/neighbors, extended family, spouse/partner, and ex-partner more than the general population of parents. Like all parents, the thing BF parents say they want most are more family experiences to attend together with their kids. In fact, BF parents say they want these experiences more than parents from any other family structure.

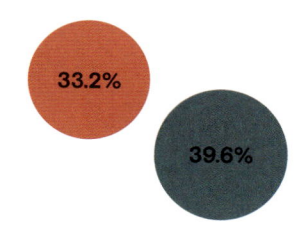

→ 33.2% of blended family parents say faith is *important* or *extremely important* for their kids, as compared to 39.6% of the general population of parents.

Distinctions for Same-Sex Couple Parents

→ To simplify reporting, we will simply use an abbreviated SS to denote two parent caregiver same-sex parents, and an abbreviated HS to denote two parent caregiver heterosexual parents.

In 2019, the U.S. Census Bureau estimated just over one million same-sex households in the U.S. While this number is still low compared to the 69.4 million heterosexual households reported to be in the U.S. the number is growing.[33] In an effort to better understand the unique experience and needs of same-sex parents, this study set out to slightly over-represent them in demographics. The final sample size for this group however, is significantly small—only 50. The findings below cannot be considered statistically significant, but may be helpful to facilitate further exploration into the unique needs of raising kids as a same-sex couple.

What Same-Sex Couple Parents Want

Like HS parents, SS parents value character development and access to opportunities more than any other parenting value in this study. SS parents demonstrated a generally greater emphasis on their parenting by rating all parenting values *important* or *extremely important* more often than HS parents. SS parents placed particular emphasis on access to resources, healthy mentors, friendship with my kid, access to opportunities, strong friendships, and balanced nutrition, rating them *important* or *extremely important* by greater than 5% more than HS parents. And most notably, SS parents say they value faith as *important* or *extremely important* 13% less often than HS parents.

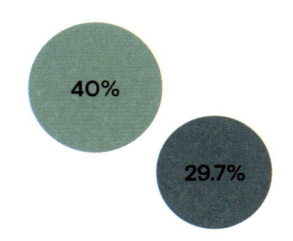

What Same-Sex Couples Fear

40%

29.7%

→ 40% of SS parents say they worry about their kids being bullied by other kids *often* or *all of the time* compared to 29.7% of HS parents.

SS parents do not differ from HS parents in their source of greatest concern: good eating habits/nutrition. But the second highest source of worry reported by SS parents is fear that their kids will be bullied. Forty percent of SS parents as opposed to 29.7% of HS parents say they worry *often* or *all of the time* about their kids being bullied by other kids. SS parents also report higher levels of worry about depression, suicide, and busyness and exhaustion for their kids. Leaders wishing to better understand the experience of SS parents' raising kids may want to take note that SS parents particularly value friendships and mentors, and worry most about bullies.

What Same-Sex Couples Feel

When it comes to the way SS parents describe themselves, SS parents do not differ from HS parents in their overall confidence. In particular,

SS parents say they are less worried and less busy than HS parents. And SS parents say they are more present/responsive and connected than HS parents. The word SS parents selected less than HS parents by greater than 10% is *supported*.

Where Same-Sex Couples Go For Help

SS parents report having consulted sources for parenting help 10% more often than HS parents. In fact, there was no source presented in this study that SS parents reported consulting less than other parents, including church. In fact, 20% of SS couples say they have consulted a church for parenting help, which may be surprising considering that SS couples both value and worry about their kids' faith less than HS parents. In particular, SS parents consulted online video, podcasts, and books more than 20% more often than HS parents.

SS parents also differed in what resources they wanted. Like all parents, SS parents say they want more family experiences to attend together with their kids, a higher percentage of SS parents (34%) than HS parents (23.4%) say they would like to have more practical training to help them prioritize their parenting efforts.

Different Ways to
Read This Book

→ This book has a lot of data. And maybe what you're looking for doesn't line up with the overarching structure of what parents want, what parents fear, how parents feel, and where parents find help. Here are a few other ways to read the findings.

If you want to know all about the average U.S. parent, only read the sub-sections about human parents.
→ Raising Humans with the Future in Mind (page 18)
→ Raising Humans in an Unpredictable World (page 34)
→ Human Parent Feelings (page 52)
→ How Human Parents Feel Supported (page 57)
→ Humans Need Help Raising Humans (page 72)

If you want to know all about how committed Christian parents compare to the average U.S. parent.
→ Levels of Enthusiasm (page 19)
→ Where the Gaps Widen (section 1, page 19)
→ Levels of Worry (page 34)
→ Where the Gaps Widen (section 2, page 36)
→ Where the Gaps Widen (section 3, page 54)
→ Levels of Support (page 58)
→ Levels of Helpfulness (page 72)
→ Where the Gaps Widen (section 4, page 76)

If you love Top-40 countdowns, Best in Show, The Greatest of All Time, only read the sub-sections with lists.
→ What Parents Want Most (page 19)
→ What Parents Fear Most (page 36)
→ What Parents Feel Most (page 53)
→ Where Parents Go for Help Most (page 73)

If you want to know more about the current status of Christian parents and their take on faith and church, check out these subsections.
→ The Importance of Faith and Church (page 23)
→ Parent Concerns about Faith and Church (page 41)
→ How Parents Feel Supported by the Church (page 61)
→ How Parents Feel Supported to Raise Kids with Faith and Character (page 62)

If you want to know more about what U.S. parents think about raising kids with strong character check out these sub-sections.
→ The Importance of Character (page 21)
→ How Parents Feel Supported to Raise Kids with Faith and Character (page 62)
→ Help for Raising Kids with Character (page 76)

If you're an age-group leader, and you want the highlights on what matters to parents at every phase, flip to the end of every section and look for:
→ What Parents Want at Every Phase (page 26)
→ What Parents Fear at Every Phase (page 44)
→ How Parents Feel at Every Phase (page 64)
→ What Helps Parents at Every Phase (page 84)

If you want quality tweetable, sharable, conversation-starters to drop into conversations and impress your friends check out the:
→ Key Findings (section 1, page 28)
→ Key Findings (section 2, page 46)
→ Key Findings (section 3, page 66)
→ Key Findings (section 4, page 86)

Want to know how to read this book with a team? You can find a free download and any additional resources at:

ThinkOrange.com/ParentResearch

Methodology
with Arbor Research

→ For the quantitative data in this report, a research team from Arbor Research Group commissioned by Orange and Parent Cue conducted four primary studies over an eighteen-month period from December 2020 through March 2022.

Each study contained a set of repeating, foundational questions to ensure the sample was weighted for and representative of known U.S. Census ethnicity, gender, age, region, and income, and each study produced a margin of error of ±3%. One qualitative study through Orange in the fall of 2021 provided additional personal reflection.

Study 1
A General Parent Study
Fall of 2020

A nationally representative sample of 571 non-religious parents completed an online survey to gather quantitative data to assess 36 virtues and their perceived significance for parenting. A qualitative analysis of the results included three consecutive conversations with a 36-person focus group.

Study 2
A General Parent Study
June 2021

A nationally representative sample of 1,464 U.S. parents completed the survey and met the primary criteria for the project. The random, anonymous, online survey was composed of approximately 35 questions. The questions included Likert type scale, max/diff, open-ended and demographic questions.

Study 3
One Christian Leader Question
Fall 2021

Additional qualitative research was performed while meeting on location with 4,697 ministry leaders. Orange invited participation in this study by asking one open-ended question for reflection. 500 Christian ministry leaders opted into the study by submitting their responses.

Study 4 and 5
A Christian Parent Study
February and March 2022

A randomly selected, nationally representative sample of 1,269 U.S. parents completed the initial and primary survey referenced in this work meeting criteria for this project as self-described "committed Christians," who report attending church at least once a month. A second survey of 847 U.S. parents following the same criteria was issued the month following. Both surveys were random, anonymous, and online; the first composed of approximately 35 questions, and the second 39 questions including Likert type scale, max/diff, open-ended and demographic questions.

Limitations

While the directors, researchers, and writers for this project have made every effort to ensure that each study followed appropriate techniques to provide academically rigorous and thorough data, no research is without assumptions and limitations. The following are a few of the assumptions made and some associated limitations.

Our Context →

This research was initiated by a team of leaders at Orange and Parent Cue, both divisions of The reThink Group Inc, whose non-profit mission is the advancement of the Church and family for the faith and future of young people. While the multi-denominational and far-reaching context of Orange serves as a primary location for asking questions about the intersection of church and family, we recognize that our location in Atlanta, GA, and our own life experience is likely to shape the approach and questions included in these studies.

The Timing →

It is well worth noting that the studies included in this publication began during a season of significant disruption due to the COVID-19 pandemic, the highly publicized murders of Ahmaud Arbery, George Floyd, and the Atlanta shooting of six Asian women, along with a highly polarized U.S. presidential election. Due to the timing of the studies, it is also mentionable that the general population study occurred ten months prior to the Christian parent population study, and the timing may limit the findings.

Correlation vs Causation →

The data in this study is not intended to demonstrate a causation relationship between faith and other aspects of parenting. All comparative data is intended to draw attention to correlations that may provide a thoughtful framework for further exploration.

Qualitative Reflection →

Christian leader participation in the open-response question was not a random, nationally representative sample. Participants were entirely composed of ministry leaders who participate with Orange and therefore are likely to have a shared set of values for family, church, and faith. Their participation is exclusively limited to the pages of this study focused on the response to this question: "What do you wish someone had done for your parent growing up that could have helped them be a better parent?" The responses submitted are not reflected in the quantitative data and reporting in any meaningful way.

Definitions of Terms →

Participants in both the general population study and Christian parent study self-reported on a variety of issues such as "bullying," "racism," and "anxiety," and participants self-reported their own feelings related to "worried" and "supported." No definition of terms was provided for these concepts. The studies sought to explore a wide range of parent perception, but the findings should be read with the assumption that parents may have varied in their interpretation of terms.

Our Choice to Trust Parents →

As mentioned at the beginning of this work, we have made the deliberate choice throughout every study to take parents at their word in a posture of trust. As a result, this study is not intended to be anything other than an opportunity to listen deeply to what parents have to say about their own experience.

For more information on how we conducted our research:
ThinkOrange.com/ParentResearch

Notes

1. Paul Taylor and Scott Keeter, editors, "Millennials: Confident. Connected. Open to Change," Pew Research Center, February 2010, 17, https://www.pewresearch.org/social-trends/2010/02/24/millennials-confident-connected-open-to-change/

2. Gretchen Livingston, "Growing Number of Dads Home with the Kids," Pew Research Center, June 5, 2014, https://www.pewresearch.org/social-trends/2014/06/05/growing-number-of-dads-home-with-the-kids/

3. Katy Steinmetz, "Help, My Parents are Millennials," Time Magazine, October 15, 2015, https://time.com/help-my-parents-are-millennials-cover-story/

4. Pew Research Center, "Parenting in America: Outlook, worries, aspirations are strongly linked to financial situation," December 17, 2015, https://www.pewresearch.org/social-trends/2015/12/17/parenting-in-america/

5. Brad Harrington, Jennifer Sabatini Fraone, Jegoo Lee, "The New Dad: The Career-Caregiving Conflict," Center for Work & Family, Boston College Carroll School of Management, 2017, 7, https://www.bc.edu/content/dam/files/centers/cwf/research/publications/researchreports/BCCWF%20The%20New%20Dad%202017.pdf

6. One 2015 study by Pew research underscores parental desire to raise kids with character in their finding that 71% of U.S. parents say it's extremely important to them that their children be honest and ethical as adults. This places character well above parents' value of their kids' future financial independence (54 percent) or ambition (45 percent).

    Pew Research Center, "Parenting in America: Outlook, worries, aspirations are strongly linked to financial situation," December 17, 2015, https://www.pewresearch.org/social-trends/2015/12/17/3-parenting-approaches-and-concerns/

7. *Guiding Children to Discover the Bible, Navigate Technology and Follow Jesus*, Barna Research Group, January 29, 2020, "58% of Highly Engaged Christian Parents Choose a Church with Their Kids in Mind," https://www.barna.com/research/children-church-home/

8. Orange and the Barna Group, Introduction by Reggie Joiner and Carey Nieuwhof, *State of the Church and Family 2010 Annual Report*, 9

9. Mark H. Freeston, Josée Rhéaume, Hélène Letarte, Michel J. Dugas, Robert Ladouceur, "Why do people worry?," *Personality and Individual Differences*, Volume 17, Issue 6, 1994, Pages 791-802, https://www.sciencedirect.com/science/article/abs/pii/0191886994900485

10. Kathryn Doyle, "Parent behaviors linked to kids' anxiety, depression," Reuters, December 3, 2015, https://www.reuters.com/article/us-parent-kids-anxiety-depression-idUSBRE9BC0VR20131213

11 The top worries cited in the Christian parent and all parent categories are similar but have two distinctions:

   Christian Parents Top Worries: Good Eating/Nutrition (46.6%), Getting Enough Sleep (45.2%), Influence of Peers (43.8%), Responsible Use of Technology (43.5%), Religious Faith (41.9%)

   All Parent Top Worries: Good Eating/Nutrition (42.8%), Getting Enough Sleep (36.9%), Anxiousness (35.6%), Responsible Use of Technology (33.8%), Being Bullied by Other Kids (32.1%)

12 Stop words are generally filtered out before processing natural language in an open-response format. They are the most common words in any language (articles, prepositions, pronouns, and conjunctions) and do not add much information to the text.

13 Vignesh Ramachandran, "Study reveals differences in how Black and white U.S. parents talked to their kids about race and racism before and after George Floyd's death," *Stanford News*, September 14, 2021, https://news.stanford.edu/2021/09/14/many-white-parents-arent-talk-race-kids/

   Claire McCarthy, "How Racism Harms Children," *Harvard Health Publishing*, January 8, 2020, https://www.health.harvard.edu/blog/how-racism-harms-children-2019091417788

   Perri Klass, "The Impact of Racism on Children's Health," *New York Times*, August 12, 2019, https://www.nytimes.com/2019/08/12/well/family/the-impact-of-racism-on-childrens-health.html

14 This section refers to Study 5 and the Follow-Up Study.

15 Parents may demonstrate strong awareness of their kids anxiety. The median age for onset of childhood anxiety is eleven according to data from the American Psychological Association.

   Kirsten Weir, "Brighter futures for anxious kids," *Monitor on Psychology*, 48(3), March 2017, http://www.apa.org/monitor/2017/03/anxious-kids

16 Jennifer Glass, Robin Simon, Matthew A Anderson, "Parenthood and Happiness: Effects at Work-Family Reconciliation Policies in 22 OECD Countries," American Journal of Sociology, Vol. 122 (3), 2016, 886-929, https://www.ncbi.nlm.nih.gov/pmc/articles/PMC5222535/

17 Carlo Schuengel, & Mirjam Oosterman. "Parenting self-efficacy." In M. H. Bornstein (Ed.), Handbook of Parenting: Being and Becoming a Parent, 2019, 654–680, Routledge/Taylor & Francis Group. https://doi.org/10.4324/9780429433214-19

18 Matthew R. Sanders, M Woolley, "The relationship between maternal self-efficacy and parenting practices: Implications for parent training." *Child: Care, Health and Development*, 2005, 31(1):65–73.

19 Anya Wittkowski, et al, "Self-Report Measures of Parental Self-Efficacy: A Systematic Review of the Current Literature," *Journal of Child and Family Studies*, Vol. 26 (11), 2017, 2960-2978 https://www.ncbi.nlm.nih.gov/pmc/articles/PMC5646137/#CR35

20. Pew Research Center, "Parenting in America: Outlook, worries, aspirations are strongly linked to financial situation," December 17, 2015, https://www.pewresearch.org/social-trends/2015/12/17/parenting-in-america/

21. This 2015 study by Pew Research demonstrates that the income gap isn't only in how parents feel supported, it's also in the kind of things parents worry about. At least half of parents with family incomes less than $30,000 worry their children might be kidnapped, beat up, or attacked. And just under half (47%) worry their child may be shot at some point, more than double the share of high-income parents.

22. 90% of Christian parents report feeling supported to well-supported in their kids faith development as opposed to 39% of the general population.

23. This data came from a smaller subset.

24. It's noteworthy that we only asked this question to the general population of parents.

    One oversight of this study was that this question was not asked specifically of Christian parents in comparison to the general population. We might make some assumptions however about how Christian parents might have responded based on their support ratings in the area of character development generally. While Christian parent responses indicated higher levels of support in the area of character development, the margin of difference was less than in other parenting areas. This suggests that Christian parents may feel more supported in their kids character development, but only marginally so.

25. "Strengthening Families: A Protective Factors Framework." *Center for the Study of Social Policy*, https://cssp.org/wp-content/uploads/2018/08/SF_Social-Connections.pdf

26. Child Welfare Information Gateway, "Brief on Protective Factors Approaches in Child Welfare," Children's Bureau/ACYF/ACF/, 2014, https://www.childwelfare.gov/pubPDFs/protective_factors.pdf

27. According to the Springtide report, having adult mentors decreases loneliness in teens and 24% of young people who have no adult mentor do not feel like their life has meaning or purpose. Just one adult mentor reduces that percentage to 6%.

    The State of Religion & Young People 2020: Relational Authority, Springtide Research, 2020, https://springtideresearch.org/annual-report-2020/?page=42

    Peter Scales, Peter Benson, Marc Mannes, "The contribution to adolescent well-being made by nonfamily adults: An examination of developmental assets as contexts and processes." *Journal of Community Psychology*, 2006, 34. 401 – 413 https://www.researchgate.net/publication/229880832_The_contribution_to_adolescent_well-being_made_by_nonfamily_adults_AN_examination_of_developmental_assets_as_contexts_and_processes

28 While the all-parent study included 25.7% of single-caregiver homes, 23% of U.S. children under the age of 18 currently live in single-parent households. This makes the U.S., the country with the highest number of single-parent households in the world.

Stephanie Kramer, "U.S. has world's highest rate of children living in single-parent households," Pew Research Center, December 12, 2019, https://www.pewresearch.org/fact-tank/2019/12/12/u-s-children-more-likely-than-children-in-other-countries-to-live-with-just-one-parent/

29 Kevin D. Dougherty, Michael O. Emerson, "The Changing Complexion of American Congregations," *Journal for the Scientific Study of Religion*, Vol. 57, Issue 1, March 2018.

For the study, Dougherty and Emerson analyzed data from the National Congregations Study, a nationally representative survey conducted in 1998, 2006-2007 and 2012, with a cumulative sample of 4,071 congregations. The study found that:

One-third of U.S. congregations were composed entirely of one race in 2012, down from nearly half of U.S. congregations in 1998.

Multiracial congregations constituted 12 percent of all U.S. congregations in 2012, up from 6 percent in 1998.

The percentage of Americans worshipping in multiracial congregations climbed to 18 percent in 2012, up from 13 percent in 1998.

Mainline Protestant and Evangelical Protestant churches have become more common in the count of multiracial congregations, but Catholic churches continue to show higher percentages of multiracial congregations. One in four Catholic churches was multiracial in 2012.

Black members have replaced Latinos as the most likely group to worship with whites. In the typical multiracial congregation, the percentage of Black members rose to nearly a quarter in 2012, up from 16 percent in 1998. Meanwhile, Latinos in multiracial congregations dropped from 22 percent in 1998 to 13 percent in 2012.

30 "Older People Projected to Outnumber Children for First Time in U.S. History," U.S. Census Bureau, March 13, 2018, https://www.census.gov/newsroom/press-releases/2018/cb18-41-population-projections.html

31 How we define Hispanic and Latino Parents:

Latino/a,
Sometimes otherwise presented Latine, or Latinx is used for the demographic quantitative data of this study to include non-Spanish speaking individuals with Latin American decent.

Hispanic
Includes all Spanish-speaking individuals, but may exclude non-Spanish speaking individuals from Latin America

Native and Indigenous races and ethnicities are not included in the quantitative portions, as the number of respondents did not meet a minimum sample size to draw meaningful data.

32   A particularly eloquent source for the description of these characteristics is Juana Bordas' book, *The Power of Latino Leadership: 10 Principles of Inclusion, Community and Contribution*, San Francisco: Berrett-Koehler Publishers, 2013.

33   Phillip Jenkins, *The Next Christendom: The Coming of Global Christianity*, Oxford: Oxford University Press, 2011

34   "U.S. Census Bureau Releases CPS Estimates of Same-Sex Households," U.S. Census Bureau, November 19, 2019, https://www.census.gov/newsroom/press-releases/2019/same-sex-households.html

---

Racial Demographic of General Population Survey Participants:

White - 79.7%
Latino - 9.6%
Black - 6.3%
East Asian - 3.9%
Biracial/Multiracial - 3.5%
Native American/Native Alaskan - 2.2%
South Asian - 1.2%
Southeast Asian - 1.2%
Native Hawaiian/Pacific Islander - 1.2%
Other - 0.7%
Middle Eastern - 0.6%

Income Demographic of General Population Survey Participants:

Value	Percent	Count
Less than $25,000	14.9%	181
$25,000 to $34,999	12.6%	153
$35,000 to $49,999	15.2%	185
$50,000 to $74,999	19.5%	237
$75,000 to $99,999	14.1%	171
$100,000 to $124,999	10.5%	127
$125,000 to $149,999	5.5%	67
$150,000 or more	7.7%	93

Acknowledgments

Research Team

Tyler Greenway, Ph.D.
Darren Kizer, Ed.D.

Terry Linhart, Ph.D.
Eric Shieh, Ph.D.

Mark Szabo, Ph.D.

Editorial Review

Dave Adamson
Molly Bell
Maddie Gorman
Stuart Hall
Mike Jeffries

Becky Kizer
Phyllis Myung
Kim Nunes
Shane Sanchez
Tim Walker

Chinwé Williams
Melanie Williams
Karen Wilson
Candice Wynn

Writing Team

Kristen Ivy *President, Orange, & CEO, Parent Cue*
Leah Jennings *Lead Editor, Parent Cue*
Mitchell McGhee *Director of Marketing, Parent Cue*
Lauren Sellers *Lead Editor, Leadership Content*

Creative Design & Production

Elizabeth Hildreth *Art Director & Designer, Parent Cue*
Mike Jeffries *Executive Director of Publishing, Orange*
Hannah Joiner *Executive Director, Parent Cue*
Afton Phillips *Executive Director of Leadership Content, Orange*
Brian Sharp *Director of Publishing Operations, Orange*
Ashley Shugart *Executive Director of Branding, Orange*

Special Thanks

Special thanks to Lilly Endowment Inc., which is providing ongoing support for continued research to help ministry leaders better support the needs of diverse families.

Arbor Research Group

Arbor Research Group is an exclusive team of research and HR experts who help organizations solve multifaceted problems using customized and collaborative projects of all types and sizes. Arbor empowers mission-driven organizations to take their next steps with confidence by helping organizations gain the quality data and rich insights they need using custom but cost-conscious methodologies.

→ arborresearchgroup.org

Project Partners

orange

Orange creates resources, curriculum, and experiences that promote the alignment of the church and the home. The name Orange is based on the idea that two combined influences make a greater impact than just two influences. When the light of the church (yellow) combines with the heart of the home (red), you get a stronger, more vibrant impact in the life of a kid (orange). Orange also believes that when the church engages every parent and caregiver at home, they help support the primary faith influence in a kid's life. Orange empowers churches to do this better through utilizing Parent Cue as a resource that can support their parents at church and at home.

Learn more about Orange → ThinkOrange.com

PARENT CUE

Parent Cue strives to share a message of hope for every parent, grandparent, guardian, and caregiver who wants to raise their kids to have a positive future. With resources for every parent, grandparent, or caregiver, Parent Cue provides parents at every phase with professional articles, books, courses, and media. Parent Cue's goal is simply to cue you with what you need when you need it, so you can be the parent you want to be. Parent Cue also believes the church has the greatest potential to be a light in communities everywhere. Often one of the greatest gifts any family can receive is personal support for a child that comes from someone outside of the family unit. Many churches offer Parent Cue resources to the parents and guardians in their community as a service and support for their families.

Discover more resources for Parents → ParentCue.org
Or download the free Parent Cue app, available for Android and iOS